More Precious Than Gold

More Precious Than Gold

"But he knoweth the way that I take: when he hath tried me, I shall come forth as gold" (Job 23:10).

"That the trial of your faith, being much more precious than of gold that perisheth, though it be tried with fire, might be found unto praise and honour and glory at the appearing of Jesus Christ" (I Pet. 1:7).

By

Lottie Beth Hobbs

HARVEST PUBLICATIONS
P.O. Box 8456
Fort Worth, Texas 76124

EIGHTH PRINTING

ISBN 0-913838-08-X

Contents

Introduction - Meet Your Friend

"WHY?" This is the most frequently asked question in every generation — by the young and old, rich and poor, well and sick. The Book of Job is an emotionally intense story of a despondent and suffering man grappling with this question, debating with himself, his fellowman and his Maker.

Thus Job becomes a brother, a kindred spirit —

To every person who has looked upon the lifeless form of a loved one and cried in anguish: "Why?"

To everyone who has experienced pain almost intolerable and asked: "Why?"

To every parent who has received the dreaded message that a beloved son would never return from the battlefield and has broken-heartedly questioned: "Why?"

To every person who has despaired in disappointment over friends and loved ones and asked: "Why?"

To all who have had their weary and wretched midnight hours.

To all who have pondered the most perplexing of all questions: "What is life? What is death? Will man live again? Is God aware of what we do? Does he care? Why do the righteous suffer while the wicked often live in seeming peace and prosperity? Why the undeserved sufferings in the world?"

Yes, in all these things, Job is our sympathetic and understanding friend. Most people think of him merely as "that old man who had a lot of boils and a lot of patience." Beyond that, they have given little thought to a life which can do so much to strengthen the faith, courage, and hope of every child of God.

"It is the greatest thing ever written with pen . . . there is nothing, I think, in the Bible or out of it with equal literary merit." This is Thomas Carlyle's appraisal of the Book of Job. From every viewpoint, it is incomparable. In form there is nothing like it. It is a drama and may be divided into scenes and characters. The scenes are vivid. The characters are strong. The subjects dealt with are the most profound ever to challenge the mind of man. Surely the opening and closing scenes are intensely dramatic and resplendent. Unlike a drama, however, the book's major section is a poetic dialogue, externally quiet and still. Job and his friends sit and talk. But even this part of the book may be called a psychological drama — a drama of the inner being, showing the violent upheavals possible within the human heart.

Who was Job? Where did he live? When did he live? Who wrote the book? Nobody knows for sure. But it is just as well, for his problems are universal, not confined to age or time or location. All we need to know is that the book came from God. This we can know. The Jews, to whom the Old Testament oracles were committed (Rom. 3:2), have always regarded it as inspired. The New Testament twice quotes the book (I Cor. 3:19; Rom. 11:35) and once refers to Job (Jas. 5:11). Such stamps the mark of divine authenticity upon it.

It will not be our purpose to enter into the arguments of the critics, or to present a highly analytical study. Rather, *our aim will be to condense and simplify the book's major thoughts in a way practical and usable for Bible classes and individual study.* In this series, the first chapter is simply a bird's-eye view of the whole story. The remaining chapters enlarge upon the points most applicable to us today.

Our finite minds can never fully comprehend the Infinite or unravel all the mysteries which challenge our thinking — this is one lesson clearly taught in the book — therefore, we certainly do not presume to do so. However, our heavenly Father has given all the light we need for a walk of faith. Then we can *trust* when we cannot *know*, and *walk* when we cannot *see.* Job learned how. He can teach us.

— Lottie Beth Hobbs

I

Stranger Than Fiction

"THERE was a man..." Simply begins the story. Then it enlarges into the most profound, soul-searching, majestic drama ever penned. It grows in intensity until it involves all of earth and heaven. In its powerful climax the Voice of Heaven speaks, showing his intense and personal involvement in man's suffering and questioning life. If it were possible to see the drama portrayed on the stage today, we would think it incredible. It is a story stranger than fiction, but truth is often stranger than fiction.

As the curtain is drawn, we see a vivid picture of both the outward and inward state of the hero. Job was at the height of all Hebrew glory, with wealth, health, pleasant family associations, honor, prestige — "the greatest of all the men of the east." More admirable, however, was the beauty of his inner being. A man "perfect and upright" — so much so that with holy pride the Lord himself said: "There is none like him in the earth." Clothed in earth's blessings and crowned with God's favor, he had everything!

The scene changes, showing a rare glimpse into the spiritual realm as God and Satan converse. One day when the sons of God came before him, Satan came too. The Almighty asked: "Where have you been?" He replied: "I have been going to and fro in the earth, walking up and down in it." "Have you considered my servant Job?" asked the Lord (1:7, 8).

He had. Satan knew Job well: his name and all about him. He could not deny his godliness, so he tried to discredit him by impugning his motives. In effect he said: "No wonder he worships and serves you; you have given him everything in the world. Just take away all he has, and he will curse you to your face." Confident of his servant's devotion, God accepted the Devil's challenge, with just one restriction: "Behold, all that he hath is in thy power; only upon himself put not forth thine hand."

The Tempter stayed in the background and sent others to do his work. Suddenly and unexpectedly he leveled calamities upon the unsuspecting man in quick succession. The Sabeans stole Job's oxen; lightning killed his sheep; the Chaldeans carried away his camels; a great whirlwind took the lives of all his children (1:13-19).

No doubt the Evil One waited intently for his victim's reaction, his moment of decision. Would he pass the test? Was God right about his servant? The answer came when the bereaved man "rent his mantle and shaved his head and fell down upon the ground and worshipped, and said, Naked came I out of my mother's womb, and naked shall I return thither: the Lord gave, and the Lord hath taken away; blessed be the name of the Lord" (1:20,21).

Satan virtually admitted his first defeat and asked permission to test further. Jehovah said: "Behold, he is in thine hand; but save his life" (2:6). If his life had been taken, there would have been no victory either for God or Satan, for right or wrong.

The Adversary's next blow was against the man himself, who was smitten with "sore boils from the sole of his foot unto his crown." As he sat in the ashes and scraped himself with a broken piece of pottery in a futile effort to alleviate his suffering, we see an unexcelled picture of complete despair, sorrow, pain and heartache.

As the sufferer sat among the ashes, *Satan dealt his master stroke.* He used Mrs. Job as his helper and worked from within the family. Ah! That *was* a blow! She was the one person who could have been a source of strength to her husband, but instead she suggested: "Why don't you renounce God and die?" (2:9).

The next scene shows the coming of three prominent men who had heard of the tragedies and "made an appointment to come and mourn with him and to comfort him." As the friends approached, they scarcely recognized the suffering man, so wretched was his appearance. They sat down with him upon the ground. For seven days and nights no one spoke a word, for they saw that his grief was very great. Sometimes silence is the best sympathy. The Talmud says that consolers were not permitted to speak until the bereaved opened the conversation.

But grief must find expression, and after seven days the stricken man began to speak. What was the message from his pulpit of ashes? Every statement pulsated with misery of both body and spirit. He bared his tormented soul, showing to the whole world the innermost thoughts of a human heart engulfed in the tumult of despair. Looking directly upon the grief, the doubts and the agony, we are drawn sympathetically to him. Why? Because in him we view our own heartaches — only magnified and intensified. He wished he had never been born. He knew not which way to turn, for he felt hedged in and forsaken by the Lord. In anguish of soul he begged for death. Bankruptcy, bereavement, boils and a berating wife! No wonder he wanted to die!

The book's major portion is a series of discussions between Job and his three friends (Eliphaz, Bildad and Zophar) as they tried to arrive at some reason for these tragedies. Their talks evidently spanned a number of months, for the afflictions lasted for months. Here was a man known far and wide as godly, upright and benevolent. Yet suddenly he found himself in the depths of all human problems. Why? Mankind is still asking, still troubled over the inequities, the undeserved sufferings in the world. The question is universal, yet personal, one which in time touches every life in some degree.

The philosophical friends turned into prosecutors. They came to sympathize but stayed to criticize, and their accusations only added to the wretched man's grief. The gist of their reasoning is this: God blesses the righteous and punishes the wicked. Therefore, they concluded that Job's intense afflictions must be the result of the most grievous sins. They exhorted him to confess his transgressions and to repent. When he insisted upon his innocence, they charged that he only added sin to sin by refusing to admit his wrongs. The friends stated many truths, but erred in their application and thus taught falsely. This is evident by the Lord's rebuke and his repudiation of their conclusions.

In Job's response, he reasoned that the heavenly Father does not mete out so much suffering in payment for so much sin, because he observed that "the tabernacles of robbers prosper, and they that provoke God are secure." Therefore, he knew something was wrong with his friends' reasoning.

Then how could his misery be accounted for? He could not understand. He longed to take his case before his Maker and talk with him about it, but he could not find him: "Oh that I knew where I might find him. I would order my cause before him and he would answer me and I would understand him." The despairing man recalled the wonderful happy years of the past. In contrast, such wretchedness had befallen him:

> The young men hold me in derision; they abhor me, they flee from me, and spare not to spit in my face; my disease binds me about as the collar on my coat . . . my kinsfolk have failed, and my familiar friends have forgotten me . . . my bone

> cleaveth to my skin and to my flesh, and I am escaped with the skin of my teeth.

Though suffering and despair enveloped him, this perplexed soul occasionally saw a ray of light breaking through the darkness. He held on to it for dear life, and uttered such words of faith and hope that we are amazed at his spiritual strength. He could not know the fulness of God's love through Christ. Yet, look at the anchors of faith and hope which firmly held his storm-tossed spirit:

> Though he slay me, yet will I trust in him (13:15).

> I know that my redeemer liveth . . . and after my skin, even this body is destroyed, then without my flesh shall I see God (19:25, 26, A.S.V.).

> But he knoweth the way that I take: when he hath tried me, I shall come forth as gold (23:10).

> My righteousness I hold fast, and will not let it go; my heart shall not reproach me so long as I live (27:6).

Job and his three friends talked and talked but still had not found answers to all their questions. *Finally Elihu spoke,* a young man who had been silently listening to their debate. The gist of his reasoning is this: God does bring calamities upon good men — not for punishment but for purification and correction, just as loving parents chastise. He declared that mere man does not have the right or power to call the Almighty before the bar of human reason and put his decisions on trial.

At the close of the young man's wisdom-filled speech, *this drama of the spirit moves to a marvelous climax with one of the most awe-inspiring of all Scriptures.* We have the glorious privilege of hearing the voice of our Creator. He did not enter into the arguments, or explain to his bewildered servant what had happened. Job never knew that he had been the central figure in a giant controversy that involved all the forces of heaven and hell.

Rather, "The Lord answered Job out of a whirlwind, and said: Who is this that darkeneth counsel by words without knowledge? Gird up now thy loins like a man; for I will demand of thee, and answer thou me" (38:1-3). With a barrage of rhetorical questions, he presented undeniable testimony of man's weakness and ignorance when contrasted with Omnipotence. In quick succession he asked many things, such as:

> **Where wast thou when I laid the foundation of the earth? declare, if thou hast understanding.**
>
> **Hast thou commanded the morning since thy days: and caused the dayspring to know his place?**
>
> **Where is the way where light dwelleth? and as for darkness, where is the place thereof?**

This magnificent passage (38-41) is unparalleled and unforgettable. It should be studied diligently by everyone, including every skeptic and atheist, for the questions are just as vital now as ever. As God continued to speak, Job was brought to an enlightened view of himself and his Maker. In humility he was ready to repent in dust and ashes for speaking words without knowledge. Eliphaz, Bildad and Zophar were rebuked and required to offer atoning sacrifices, and Job was appointed their intercessor.

The last scene is one of joy and beauty, tranquility and triumphant faith. "The Lord gave Job twice as much as he had before."

Do you remember how frightened you sometimes became as a child when you were awakened suddenly by a severe storm? The darkness, the lightning, the thunder, the rain. All seemed so ominous, and you thought the night and the turmoil would never pass. Can you remember, too, how you felt the next morning when you awakened to look upon a world washed, purified and flooded with sunlight? How beautiful! With beauty and refreshment not possible without the storm.

This is the way we feel at the close of Job's life. We marvel at the brightness of the morning sun as it rises upon a life which has been refreshed and strengthened. We have a sense of relief. The hero, weary and battle-scarred from his bout with the Adversary, lives to smile again and to enjoy days of peace and prosperity, friendships and family ties. Truly he emerged from the crucible of trial with riches more precious than gold — a faith tested and proved — and enjoyed life on a higher, holier and happier plane than he had ever known before.

Reading the Book of Job is an emotional experience. The first emotion we feel is pity for this unfortunate man. As the drama unfolds, the pity gives way to admiration — admiration for one who is able to look upward, to attach his spirit to the Spirit above and say in effect: "Here I take my stand. Nothing else matters. Come what may, my confidence is unmoved." Our admiration blends into awe and reverence as we hear God's words. This leads to strength and encouragement and joy as we realize that the All-powerful Force who watched over Job, One so personally interested in his struggles, also watches over his children today.

BRIEF OUTLINE OF THE BOOK

I. JOB'S FIRST STATE (1:1-5).
II. SATAN PERMITTED TO TEST HIS FAITH (1:6 - 2:10).
III. A SERIES OF DISCUSSIONS BETWEEN JOB AND THREE FRIENDS.
  (1) First cycle of speeches (4 - 14).
  (2) Second cycle of speeches (15 - 21).
  (3) Third cycle of speeches (22 - 31).
IV. THE SPEECH OF ELIHU (32 - 37).
V. GOD TALKS WITH JOB (38 - 41).
VI. JOB'S RESTORATION (42:7-17).

REVIEW EXERCISE

1. Give a description of Job's spiritual condition. ....

2. He had .... sons and .... daughters.

3. Give an inventory of his material wealth. ....

....

....

4. (T or F) Satan declared that Job was not a righteous man.

5. What permission did God first grant to Satan? ....

....

6. What calamities befell Job in his first testing? ....

....

7. What was his reaction? ....

8. What was the second permission granted to Satan? ....

....

9. Why was Job's life spared? ....

....

10. What did he do to try to relieve his physical suffering? ....

....

11. Who came to comfort him? ....

12. Who finally spoke first?............ After how long a silence?............

13. (T or F) God told Job all about his conversation with Satan.

14. What is a potsherd? ....

FOR THOUGHT OR DISCUSSION

1. If Job had known all the reasons behind his severe testing, could he have proved his full devotion to God?
2. When Job's trials came, he stood at one of the major crossroads of life. His decision determined the whole of his future, here and hereafter. Name some of life's crossroads, times when one decision can have such far-reaching consequences.

II

Golden Years

A LITTLE girl said: "Tell me a happy story. I don't like the ones that make me sad." So it is with most of us. The story of Job begins with happiness — an idyllic and heart-warming scene. He had everything one could desire, including the highest praise of heaven, for God said: "There is none like him in the earth" (1:8). Wouldn't it be wonderful to receive such a compliment? What about a man worthy of such superlatives? Let's examine his treasures one by one.

The Treasure of God's Personal Concern

"My servant Job." So spoke God. These three words speak volumes, comforting volumes of admiration, affection and personal awareness. The heavenly Father knew him by name and understood every aspect of his life. Throughout the trial, he was very near and was more concerned over his child's victory than anyone else.

Every life is an object of interest in heaven. God is keenly aware of each of us, knowing us by name. Many Scriptures confirm this comforting fact. Hagar was called by name (Gen. 21:17). Our Creator knows even those who refuse to follow him, for of Cyrus it was said: "I have called thee by thy name: I have surnamed thee, though thou hast not known me" (Isa. 45:4). Never think that he is too busy running the universe to know his servants personally. He follows every detail of your life and is as concerned over your battle with Satan as he was Job's. No mother — feeling the pulse, watching the fever, only too eager for the health of a beloved — is more solicitous over a child's welfare than he.

THE TREASURE OF DIVINE APPROVAL

This was Job's most precious treasure. Without it, all other possessions would have been vain and worthless. Though the Lord knows each one, whether righteous or wicked, not everyone enjoys divine approval. Job did. The Father's personal examination resulted in the highest possible commendation: "There is none like him in the earth." Yes, Job was truly a V. I. P. Not just in the eyes of his fellowman but, above all, in the estimation of God. He was proud of Job, and all the more after his servant had gone through the fire of testing and had come forth as gold.

I think that God is proud of those who bear
A sorrow bravely — proud indeed of them
Who walk straight through the dark to find him there,
And kneel in faith to touch his garment's hem.
Oh, proud of them who lift their heads to shake
Away tears from eyes that have grown dim,
Who tighten quivering lips and turn to take
The only road they know that leads to him.

How proud he must be of them — he who knows
All sorrow, and how hard grief is to bear!
I think he sees them coming, and he goes
With outstretched arms and hands to meet them there.
And with a look, a touch on hand or head,
Each finds his hurt heart strangely comforted.

— Grace Noll Crowell

The Lord is either proud or ashamed of all his servants. Of some it is said: "Wherefore, God is not ashamed to be called their God" (Heb. 11:16), implying that of some he is so ashamed that he does not even want to claim them. How did Job gain such heavenly esteem? Let's continue the inventory of his possessions.

THE TREASURE OF RIGHTEOUSNESS

When the Father described Job, he began with the most

important part, his inner being: "perfect and upright, and one that feared God, and eschewed evil" (1:1). The word righteousness is sometimes rather vague in our minds. What does it mean? To keep divine commandments, or course, but it helps to analyze it further. What made Job so righteous that he deserved the commendation of the Almighty? He worshipped the Lord (1:5) and was so careful to keep his commandments that he regarded "the words of his mouth more than my necessary food" (23:12). He abstained from sins of impurity (31:1-11) and kept his heart free of avarice and covetousness (31:24,25) and hatred (31:29,30) and deceit (27:4). He helped and comforted the widows and orphans, the poor, the sick and the weak (29:12-16) and withstood every temptation which attends great material wealth. He watched his words and kept his speech pure (27:4). James says that one who is able to bridle his tongue is a perfect man (Jas. 3:2). How true!

No wonder God described him as "perfect and upright." We are commanded to be perfect, and thus must know what is enjoined upon us (Matt. 5:48; Col. 4:12). Does it mean absolute sinlessness? No, it cannot mean this, for Job admitted his weaknesses; and John tells us that all Christians sin (I Jno. 1:8-10). Though man cannot be sinless, our heavenly Father cannot require less than perfection; to do so would give man an imperfect goal. The high standard which he has set reminds us of the constant need for improvement.

Why, then, was Job called perfect? He had so matured spiritually that his whole life was regulated by the Lord's will. That was the constant intention of his heart, and for his failures, he made amends by the atoning sacrifices. To reach spiritual maturity, one must put away childish traits and behave like an adult (I Cor. 13:11; I Cor. 16:13). Job exemplified the spirit of these commands. Immaturity would have rendered him incapable of weathering the storms ahead of him. The heroic heart demands maturity, for the immature person can neither stand severe trials nor achieve great things. Growing up and growing close to God are the best fortifications against the tribulations of the future. When Job's trials came, they found him living close to the Lord.

The dictionary defines upright as "just, honest, strictly honorable," but think further upon the uprightness of our hero. He was not always up — sometimes he was terribly down, but he didn't stay down. He got back up. He was not always right — sometimes he was wrong, but he didn't stay wrong. He got back right. Surely he was an upright man in every way. If he could do it, so can we.

THE TREASURE OF A SWEET FAMILY RELATIONSHIP

Children are gifts from God, and Job had seven sons and three daughters. They had such an enjoyable family relationship that "his sons went and feasted in their houses, every one his day; and sent and called for their three sisters to eat and drink with them" (1:4). "His day" probably refers to each birthday which became an occasion for a family celebration. Can't you imagine what a big time they must have had, when all the children and grandchildren gathered in? Surely this was one of grandfather Job's richest joys. A close and meaningful family association is one of the foretastes of heaven, for there the Father's children will be gathered around him in joy and peace.

How blessed were the children to have such a father. As priest and mediator for his whole family, he was so concerned about their souls' welfare that he arose early in the morning and offered sacrifices in their behalf — not only for known sins, but also for sins of the heart seen only by God (1:5). No effort was too great to insure the spiritual health of his family.

It is hard to estimate the power and influence of godly parents. Many times the memory of such has been a restraining and elevating force which furnished the extra strength needed by sons and daughters in critical moments of decision.

THE TREASURE OF MATERIAL WEALTH

Job was godly though wealthy, and wealthy though godly. Piety and prosperity do not always go together, but such is surely possible. The Father had abundantly blessed him (1:3), for it is he who "giveth us richly all things to enjoy" (I Tim. 6:17). Godly men can do without wealth, but wealthy men cannot do without God. Job knew this.

Poverty brings its pains and temptations. *Prosperity also tempts and tries.* Wealth often does more to a man than it does for him, because it can lull the soul to sleep in its comforts. "Gold is tested by fire, man by gold" — Chinese Proverb. Surely pitfalls threaten both the rich and the poor (Prov. 30:7-9; I Tim. 6:17). Our lives will always be a struggle between the outward and the inward; and the outward, whatever our circumstances, threatens to get the better of us. We admire a man who battles all the problems of poverty and yet remains righteous. So should we admire a man who struggles with the problems of prosperity and still remains faithful. So few do. Job was among those few.

THE TREASURE OF HEALTH

Usually we do not know what a valuable and irreplaceable treasure this is until it's too late. Most likely Job could not fully appreciate it, until the day came that disease put an end to his daily activities and rendered him incapable of any useful work.

John wrote to his good friend Gaius: "Beloved, I wish above all things that thou mayest prosper and be in health, even as thy soul prospereth" (III Jno. 2). This includes nearly everything, doesn't it?

THE TREASURE OF MANY FRIENDS

Friends are a necessary part of the good life, for man is a social being with an innate desire for meaningful and comforting associations with others. One of life's most cherished blessings is the sharing of joys and sorrows with kindred spirits. So many times we need a sympathetic ear, a guiding counsel and even a restraining hand from those dear enough to care.

> **Friendship — pure, unselfish friendship,**
> **All through life's allotted span,**
> **Nurtures, strengthens, widens, lengthens,**
> **Man's affinity with man.**

Job had many friends because he had a benevolent heart and a helpful hand. "A man that hath friends must show himself friendly" (Prov. 18:24). Prosperity makes friends and adversity tests them. When the sun is shining and all of life is gay, it is not possible to know true friends from false ones. Job did not until the testing time came. He had befriended many. He probably enjoyed the sweet delusion that all men were his friends and none his enemies. However, when the stormclouds gathered, most of them scattered like chickens in the rain — we might say they really "chickened out!"

The record tells of only four who cared enough to stand by him. How dear their friendship must have been. Three of them erred in their efforts, but they must be commended for honestly trying to render consolation. They "made an appointment together" (2:11-13). It was no accident. Nor was it aid which cost them nothing. It required personal sacrifice and inconvenience. Evidently they came great distances. They left their own work and spent several months trying to help their good friend. "The light of friendship is like the light of phosphorous, seen plainest when all around is dark" — Crowell. Only in adversity can one learn how priceless a loyal friend is. Later as Job was living in the shadow of death, he begged for sympathy and understanding from his friends (19:21,22). He needed them more than ever before.

> When the silver cord is fraying
> And the voice must soon be still
> Loving ties are tensed to breaking
> Bowing to the Father's will —
> When the curtained doors have welcomed
> Life beginning, not its end,
> And we grope in tearful silence —
> It is then we need a friend.

THE TREASURE OF HONOR AND PRESTIGE

Within every heart is a desire for approval. No person enjoys disfavor, but rather longs for his fellowman's favor. Christ understands this full well. As he grew to manhood, he "increased in wisdom and stature, and in favor with God and man" (Lk. 2:52). At one time he enjoyed such popularity that the people sought to make him their earthly king (Jno. 6:15). Later, however, he experienced such disfavor that fickle and envious men put him to death.

Job could tell us, too, how it feels to receive from his fellowman both the highest possible honor and the most foul dishonor. During his days of prosperity and popularity, young men regarded him almost with veneration, and older men looked upon him with such respect that they stood in his presence. Noblemen and princes gave heed to his counsel (29:7-11). Days of honor, favor and prestige were his.

THE BEST OF TWO WORLDS

Surely these were blessed years. How old was Job at this time? Evidently middle-aged, for his children were grown and yet men older than his father were still living (15:10). In the prime of life, he possessed the best of two worlds —

the sunlight of divine favor surrounded him, as he tasted the sweet joys of earth.

Are we to suppose that no ripple ever marred the calm of his daily sea? Certainly not, for he had been through all the problems which attend child-rearing, the tensions and responsibilities of supporting a family, and all the ups and downs which are a part of living. Yet no major tragedy had befallen him. Whatever his frustrations and distresses, they were small in comparison with the tribulations which yet faced him. Until real trouble comes, it is easy to imagine trivial things to be trouble.

We look upon Job's happy and tranquil state and wish that it could always remain so. We are like the little girl who said: "Tell me a happy story." This is a happy story. Though our hero went through dark and discouraging days, we can follow him through the storm and out into the peaceful sunlight again. This is the important thing. Every life ends happily and successfully, if it ends with the crown of God's favor. Job's life did.

REVIEW EXERCISE

1. What compliment did God bestow upon Job? ....

....

2. Give at least one Scripture which shows that God knows each person by name. ....

3. What did John wish for his friend Gaius? ....

....

4. To what sins does poverty tempt one, as stated in Proverbs?

....

5. In the same Scripture, what temptations are specified concerning wealth? ....

6. What had Job done in the past to help others? ....

....

....

7. How much honor did Christ at one time enjoy among his fellow-men? ....

8. (T or F) It is impossible to be both wealthy and godly.

9. "A man that hath friends must ...."

FOR THOUGHT OR DISCUSSION

1. "My servant Job." These three words tell much about God. What do they tell about Job?

2. When Joseph was tempted by Potiphar's wife, his firm conviction that he must not sin against God restrained him (Gen. 39:9). Though he was many miles from home, was this strong faith a living testimony of the influence his godly parents still wielded in his life?

3. How much concern do most parents today have over the spiritual welfare of their children? Give some specific reasons for your answers.

4. Try to imagine what God would say if he were to describe you to Satan today. Would he be proud or ashamed?

5. Before Job's trials, do you think it was possible for him to appreciate fully the blessings of health, prosperity, friends and a wonderful family relationship? If you have these joys, try to be as grateful as possible each day — for time inevitably brings changes.

6. In our effort to be perfect, we must first be cleansed by Christ's blood. Then what must we do to enjoy a continual cleansing? (I Jno. 1:7).

III

Stronger Than Satan

ONE day a little boy asked his mother: "If God drowned all the bad things in the flood, why didn't he drown the Devil too?" Before the mother had time to reply, he continued: "Oh, I know why. Because the Devil is a spirit, and I guess he could creep aboard the ark too, if he wanted to, couldn't he?" With his simple childish faith, he was far wiser than many who hold college degrees; for it has become fashionable in many circles to deny the reality of Satan. Even some who stand in pulpits either deny his existence or declare that belief in him has no real bearing on our lives. It has this much bearing: the person who becomes a devil-denier soon has little or no religion at all. Why? One who rejects the reality of Satan also rejects the reality of hell. Then, if there is nothing to be saved *from,* what is the sense of a doctrine of salvation? The devil-denier is thus stripped of all motivation toward righteousness and all restraint against evil. He is also baffled by the enigma of evil. He cannot deny its presence in the world, but he has no explanation of its origin, its nature or its conquest.

Many who deny the existence of Satan and hell claim to believe in God and heaven. This is highly inconsistent, for the same Bible which teaches one teaches them all.

The Evil One is real — an intelligent, crafty, diligent and powerful Personality. He is one of the major characters in Job's questioning and suffering life, and also in yours. It is not possible to understand Job's life or our lives without considering the part he plays.

THE MANY FACES OF SATAN

You have heard of one who is two-faced, meaning hypocritical. The Devil is the original hypocrite. He has more than two faces. There are so many views of his many-sided personality that it is difficult always to recognize him.

His conversations give us several aspects of his personality. He talked with Eve (Gen. 3:1-5). He talked with Christ (Matt. 4:1-11). He talked with God (1:7-12; 2:1-6), and thereby revealed much concerning his nature and work. "Now when the sons of God came to present themselves before the Lord, and Satan came also among them" (1:6). No one knows for sure the nature of this meeting. "Sons of God" is a term applied both to men (Gen. 6:2) and to angels (38:7). However, Satan had been cast out of heaven, and we have no record of his again having the privilege of assembling with the hosts of heaven. Therefore, "sons of God" may refer to God's children on earth as they assembled for a worship service. Whatever this meeting was, both God and Satan were present. Their conversation reveals both to be intelligent Personalities.

SATAN, YOUR ADVERSARY

You may not spend much time thinking about the Devil; but remember — he surely thinks about you. Whether you realize it or not, he is at war with you. He is your enemy. He desires your downfall. It is only smart to learn as much as possible about your opponent.

He works here on earth among us. When God asked, "Whence cometh thou?" he answered: "From going to and fro in the earth and walking up and down in it" (1:7). This is his own description, and from it we immediately sense his nearness to us and perceive his restless, ceaseless, vigilant motion.

He is a diligent personal worker. God asked: "Hast thou

considered my servant Job?" He had! He knew him by name and had already examined him fully and formed his conclusions. Thus, he is not some abstract force. He deals with each life individually. He knows us by name. Knows our strengths and weaknesses. We are warned: "Be sober, be vigilant; because your adversary the devil, as a roaring lion, walketh about, seeking whom he may devour" (I Pet. 5:8). If he were not a real and ever-present threat, there would be no sense to this warning. He is busy seeking souls, testing to see "whom he may devour."

He works chiefly among the righteous. Why? The wicked already belong to him. A lion does not chase the prey which he already possesses. Therefore, the closer one is to God, the harder the Adversary works on him. Job was the most righteous person on earth at that time. Satan controlled most of the world — he always has — so why didn't he leave this one man alone? Simply because he was so righteous. If the Tempter could have succeeded in turning this spiritual giant away from God, think what a victory it would have been.

The life of Peter bears testimony of the Wicked One's shrewd personal awareness and his efforts to sabotage the faith of each child of God. On one occasion Christ said: "Simon, Simon, behold, Satan hath desired to have you, that he may sift you as wheat" (Lk. 22:31).

This is further demonstrated in the life of Christ. Satan got on his trail right after his baptism and followed him all the way to the cross. If Christ was such a target, can his followers expect to escape his darts? No one can be at peace with God without being at war with the Devil. This means that the righteous will always be at variance with all his agents. It is a lifelong battle, and for this reason it is impossible not to have some enemies in the fight. Though he had done no wrong, Christ had enemies who finally took his life. So did Paul. So did Peter.

NO ENEMIES?

He has no enemies you say?
My friend, your boast is poor:
He who hath mingled in the fray
Of duty, that the brave endure
Must have made foes. If he has none,
Small is the work that he has done.
He has hit no traitor on the hip,
He has cast no cup from tempted lip.
He has never turned the wrong to right.
He has been a coward in the fight.

SATAN, THE FALSE ACCUSER

Slandering and falsely accusing good men originated with the Devil. This instigated the controversy surrounding Job and became the cause of his trials.

The challenge. When God asked if he had considered Job, Satan replied with an accusation. In effect, he accused the godly man of serving his Maker only for mercenary reasons: "Doth Job fear God for nought? ... But put forth thine hand now, and touch all that he hath, and he will curse thee to thy face" (1:9-11). Thus Satan issued to God a challenge to prove his servant's fidelity and godliness.

The challenge accepted. God granted the permission: "Behold all that he hath is in thy power" (1:12). Why would he grant such power? Was he allowing the Evil One the pleasure of making diabolical sport of Job, as the Philistines did of the blind Samson? No. Satan had made a false charge against the most righteous man on earth. Though we do not presume to know all the reasons, it served the purpose of proving to devils, to angels and to all mankind that there is such a thing as unselfish goodness and indestructible faith.

Therefore, the test was evidently not for Job's benefit alone, but also for our edification and encouragement.

Our Adversary's role as false accuser is mentioned again in Revelation; he is pictured as "the accuser of our brethren, who accuses them before our God day and night" (Rev. 12:10). His followers are most adept in this art even to this day. Evil beings are determined to find evil in others, even when there is none. They judge everyone by themselves and attribute to others the depraved motives in their own hearts.

SATAN, THE WRECKER

The Devil specializes in tearing down every good thing. He was trying to do this to Job — to wreck a faithful life through agonizing hardships.

"And he showed me Joshua the high priest standing before the angel of the Lord, and Satan standing at his right hand to resist him" (Zech. 3:1). Wherever the Lord's servants are, the Adversary's agents are near, ready to resist and, if possible, to wreck every good work — whether by persecution (II Tim. 3:12) or by false doctrines (Acts 20:28-30) or by strife and confusion (Jas. 3:16).

SATAN, THE DECEIVER

The world's Great Deceiver can change color quicker than a chameleon and appear to be anything which suits his purpose. Some people think they have never met him, simply because they do not know how to recognize him. He never appears in his true light, ugly and repulsive, but rather comes most often in very attractive forms.

He makes sin look appealing. How did he beguile Eve (II Cor. 11:3)? By holding before her the beautiful, desirable and enticing: "And when the woman saw that the tree was good for food, and that it was pleasant to the eyes, and a tree to be desired to make one wise, she took of the fruit thereof" (Gen. 3:6). That was the bait; the Great Deceiver did not show her the hook inside — the fears, tears, heartaches and death.

He transforms himself into an angel of light (II Cor. 11: 13,14) and as such works in the realm of religion, teaching his doctrines (I Tim. 4:1), operating his churches (Rev. 2:9; 3:9), blinding the minds of men (II Cor. 4:4), and stealing God's word from their hearts (Lk. 8:12).

The Devil works through people. This is one of the most deceiving aspects of his personality. He used the Sabeans, the Chaldeans, Job's wife and his friends. At no time did the suffering man realize the part the Great Deceiver was playing in his life. He was an unseen adversary, and the perplexed man seemed to be boxing a shadow, wearing himself out but getting practically nowhere. Was he? No. He was winning, though he did not fully understand the battle. Because of his conquest, we can better know the Adversary. Judas served as Satan's agent (Lk. 22:3). Even Christ's beloved friend Peter allowed himself to become a satanic tool upon one occasion (Matt. 16:23). How does one do this? Anytime he helps promote one of the goals of the Devil, whether by hindering good or encouraging evil.

SATAN, THE TEMPTER

The word tempt means to entice, to try to lure one into. Satan is called the tempter (I Thess. 3:5). As the father of all sin (I Jno. 3:8; Jno. 8:44), his goal is to lure everyone into the evil of which he is guilty.

Every weapon he had was used against Job. You will never be required to resist a temptation or bear a sorrow which he did not meet and conquer. As the story opens, he had already withstood all the temptations of prosperity. Then the Tempter tested him with adversity. Some can faithfully endure adversity, only to turn away from God in prosperity, as the children of Israel did. Others who stand in prosperity fall in times of adversity. Job withstood the pressures and trials of both.

Satan's persistence is so evident. When one effort failed on Job, he immediately tried something else. So it was with Christ. After his baptism, the Wicked One appeared and offered his devilish appeals, "And when the devil had ended all the temptation, he departed from him for a season" (Lk. 4:13) "For a season." He always returns.

STRONGER THAN SATAN?

The Tempter roams the earth as a privileged Being. He rules most of the world, being called the prince of this world and the god of this world. The throngs which rally behind him today are popular, and in many cases well-organized and well-financed. It may seem unfair that he and all his forces should be unleashed upon one lone man such as Job — or on each of us — and that each person has the problem of being stronger than Satan. Can man succeed? Of course. He not only can, but he must. Being unconquerable is not only possible but absolutely necessary, or else one will share his eternal destiny (Matt. 25:41).

THE LIMITATIONS OF HIS POWER

Since the Devil is so powerful, it is encouraging to understand the limitations of his power. Are we merely as helpless putty in his diabolical hands? Not at all.

Satan's power is limited by God. Though the Almighty does not endorse or desire what the Devil does, he grants to him freedom within limitations. He could test Job only so far (1:12; 2:6). Our Father has promised that we will not be tempted above what we are able to bear (I Cor. 10:13).

> He will allow no grief imposed
> Beyond the strength that He bestows.

Our Adversary's power is limited by Christ, who triumphed over him completely. He not only resisted every temptation (Heb. 4:15), but also broke his power by triumphing over death (Heb. 2:14). If we follow in Christ's steps, we can also be victorious.

His power is limited by man. Though the Tempter may bring hardships upon us, he cannot do anything within us except that which we permit him to do. He cannot enter man's heart and control him against his will. If so, he would have done this to Job. Man has a freedom of will. He can resist Satan's force, no matter how violent or frequent his attacks may be (Jas. 4:7). Job did — and proved to God, to Satan, to you and me, that righteous people of all time can do the same. The All-powerful One will help to deliver out of temptation (II Pet. 2:9), but man must make the first move. "Draw nigh to God, and he will draw nigh to you" (Jas. 4:8). Every trial and temptation furnishes an opportunity for us to draw nearer to God.

"Your adversary the devil" constantly seeks "whom he may devour," but he cannot devour everyone. As powerful as he is, man can be stronger — for God is stronger than Satan. Thus, any person who stays with God has the balance of power with him, though all the forces of earth and hell should be against him. Job was stronger than Satan. We can be!

REVIEW EXERCISE

1. How does Peter describe the devil? ....

   .... Scripture: ....

2. What challenge did Satan issue to God? ....

   ....

3. .... accuses the brethren "before our God day and night." Scripture: ....

4. What characteristics of Satan are given in John 8:44? ....
....

5. "................................... the devil, and he will flee from you." Scripture: ....

6. (T or F) Satan knew Joshua personally.

7. Acts 20:28-30 is speaking of the Lord's church. When a Christian begins to teach a false doctrine, whose agent does he become?
....

8. (T or F) At the time Satan appeared to Eve, there was no person through whom he could work and he thus took the form of a serpent.

9. What is the devil's eternal destiny? ....
Scripture: ....

10. Name some Biblical examples of people who allowed themselves to be used as instruments of Satan. ....
....

11. What did Christ say the Devil desired to do with Peter? ....
.... Scripture: ....

FOR THOUGHT OR DISCUSSION

1. Temptations vary with different ages and circumstances. What do you think to be some of the most prevalent temptations facing young people? Middle-aged people? Older people?

2. Does Satan actually talk to us today? How does he do this?

3. No matter how unjust a thing may be, or how directly it may come from Satan, is it possible for the trial to be turned into a blessing for us?

IV

The Tempest Outside

SOMETIMES trials come gradually. They appear first as a small and innocent-looking speck on the horizon and then grow in size and intensity until a black cloud envelops our whole world. This can be true of illness, domestic heartaches, church troubles, national turbulence and other burdens. Oftentimes, however, the storm strikes suddenly with little or no warning.

Think of the unfortunate man in the story of the Good Samaritan. More than likely he got up one morning as usual, ate breakfast, kissed his family good-bye and started unsuspectingly on his journey. Before night, calamities had leveled him. He lay almost beaten to death, robbed, alone and friendless. Life can get rough in a hurry.

Job, too, got up one morning as usual. Before night had come, a storm had descended upon him which seemed greater than he could bear. He said: "For he breaketh me with a tempest" (9:17). Consider the things which happened *to* him. In the next chapter, we shall look at the storm which raged *within* him.

He Lost Material Possessions

Satan's first stroke was to wipe out Job's material wealth (1:14-17). At this point, he still had his family and friends and health. Materially he had as much as he started with (I Tim. 6:7). If his Adversary had stopped there, the stricken man could have recovered his losses. Many people have.

Families who have suffered severe financial reverses realize what a trial this can be. Though material things are relatively unimportant, their sudden loss has caused many to doubt God's love and goodness. Others have turned from him completely. Still others have despaired of life and died at their own hands. The Adversary knew what a temptation this would be, or he would not have tried it on Job.

DEATH TOOK ALL HIS CHILDREN

Death's stern shock has caused some to renounce God, and thus the Devil's next effort was to take from Job all ten children at once (1:18,19).

PHYSICAL SUFFERING OVERWHELMED HIM

It is difficult to imagine a disease so completely devastating as that which afflicted Job. His own description of his pitiful condition vibrates with unexcelled misery:

> My flesh is clothed with worms and clods of dust; my skin is broken and become loathsome (7:5).
>
> My bone cleaveth to my skin and to my flesh, and I am escaped with the skin of my teeth (19:20).
>
> My bones are pierced in me in the night season: and my sinews take no rest. By the great force of my disease is my garment changed: it bindeth me about as the collar of my coat (30:17,18).
>
> My skin is black upon me, and my bones are burned with heat (30:30).

Have you ever sat by the bed of one so immersed in pain that he begged for the release which only death can bring? If so, you can partially understand Job's condition — partially, for no person can feel his brother's pain as acutely as his own. Only one who has actually experienced pain indescribably intense and prolonged can sympathize with this phase of the man's trials.

HIS WIFE TURNED AGAINST HIM

With blow after blow against this good man, Satan beat him into a pitiful, repulsive, sorrowing, suffering mass of humanity. *Next in his diabolical strategy, he wielded a real stroke of genius* by using the man's wife in an effort to land the knock-out blow. There is only one verse concerning this woman, but it speaks volumes. Oftentimes it takes only one statement to furnish an index to one's whole character. Mrs. Job placed herself on the side of Satan and against her husband. How do we know? There is no other conclusion, for she suggested the very thing the Tempter was trying to get her husband to do: "Renounce God and die" (2:9). She allowed herself to become the Devil's instrument. Now we can see why he had spared her life. If she had died along with the children, the grieving man could have comforted himself by believing that she would have stood by him. As it was, she lived to prove that she was actually an enemy in his own household. Burying her would have been easier. Many things are worse than death.

Why was this such a master satanic stroke?

Because our strongest temptations can come through those we love the most. They have the greatest influence for either good or evil. When that pull is downward, even good men may be pulled from the skies. Dryden aptly expressed it:

> He raised a mortal to the skies,
> She drew an angel down.

Job did resist, however. His reply to his wife was not harsh; yet it was a rebuke and a firm repudiation of her suggestion: "Thou speakest as one of the foolish women speaketh" (2:10). Why was her suggestion foolish? The man had already lost everything — everything! That is, except one. That was his hold upon God, his faith which linked him to heaven. Then his companion tried to get him to sever that hold, cut that link. Such would have sent him hurtling into the abyss of eternal destruction. Of course, she was foolish. Foolish with a perverted understanding. A fool has been defined as one who has missed the proportion of things, which was surely Mrs. Job's plight. Even in the midst of grief and pain, however, Job's judgment and sense of values held firm. He quickly and clearly perceived the folly of his wife's thinking.

This was a wounding stroke because those we love can hurt us the deepest. Though Job resisted her suggestion, can you sense his pain of heart as the woman who was the mother of his children aligned herself with his Enemy and enemies? He said: "They whom I have loved are turned against me" (19:19). The wound was deep. Just as those we love can injure us the most, it is possible for us to hurt our loved ones. We do not know the author of this poem, but it is worthy of careful thought:

> There's one sad truth in life I've found,
> While journeying east and west —
> The only folks we really wound
> Are those we love the best.
> We flatter those we scarcely know,
> We please the fleeting guest,
> And deal full many a thoughtless blow
> To those who love us best.

Discouragement is one of Satan's strongest weapons because encouragement is one of mankind's most basic needs. The Tempter was well aware of this. All of creation needs and responds to encouragement. Animal trainers pet and reward their charges with kindnesses and delicacies for acts of obedience. Children glow with delight when they are praised. Dr. Henry H. Goddard, a psychologist, used an instrument called the "ergograph" to measure fatigue on a group of tired children. When they were given a word of praise, the machine showed an immediate increase in energy. When the same children were scolded, the machine showed a marked sag in their energy.

Wives are either a source of encouragement or discouragement to their husbands. In *The Christian Woman,* June, 1967, is a very fine article by Mrs. James O. Baird, entitled "Words That Build." With permission, we quote excerpts:

> Husbands can be defeated or can be helped to succeed by the words of their wives. The wife who defeats her husband can do it in several ways.
>
> (1) *She can nag.* Her nagging may take the form of always demanding more than the husband can supply materially. "Why can't we have a new car?" "Why do I have to live with this dirty carpet another year?" It may be the type that always finds fault with her husband's personal habits. "Why can't you learn to put away your own clothes?" "Must you always leave the paper in a mess?" "Will you never learn to clean the mud off your shoes before coming in the house?" "Why do you always look so sloppy on Saturdays?"
>
> It may be merely used as an irritant. "You never talk to me anymore." "I thought you were going to mow the lawn today," or "I wish *I* had time to read the paper."
>
> (2) *She can depreciate him . . .*
>
> (3) *She can build her own image at the expense of his . . .*
>
> (4) *She may be silent when he needs encouragement.* A man faces many challenges during the course of a day and often faces defeat. He may come home in the evening completely disheartened and undone. A word of encouragement is all he needs to face the problem again tomorrow, but if the wife is so insensitive that she fails to give this word, defeat may become habitual for him.
>
> Encouragement from wives should cover every facet of living. Spiritual encouragement should have first priority.

Each of us needs encouragement, and the need is great; but when it does not come, we must go on without it. We cannot afford to give up. Too much is at stake. When Job tottered on the brink of total mental and physical collapse and needed encouragement more than ever before, he received nothing but discouragement. But he held on and leaned more heavily upon the Lord. Together they triumphed.

HIS CLOSE FRIENDS FALSELY ACCUSED HIM

The three friends came to comfort. No wonder Job called them "miserable comforters" (16:1-7), for they actually added to his discomfort. He looked to them for help and sympathy, but instead they chided and accused. "How long will ye vex my soul, and break me in pieces with words?" he asked (19:2). We can feel with him the agonizing cry: "Have pity upon me, have pity upon me, O ye my friends" (19:21).

They declared: "Know therefore that God exacteth of thee less than thine iniquity deserveth" (11:6). He challenged them to specify their charges, and they replied: "Thou hast taken a pledge from thy brother for nought, and stripped the naked of their clothing. Thou hast not given water to the weary to drink, and thou hast withholden bread from the hungry... Thou hast sent widows away empty, and the arms of the fatherless have been broken" (22:5-9). They stated the charges, but to state a thing does not make it so. This is something many people have not learned!

Were the accusations true? No. How do we know? Job understood full well the seriousness of sin (10:14,15) and stood ready to make amends for any error (10:2; 31:5,6), but he maintained his innocence. This alone would not exonerate him, but God himself placed the badge of innocence upon him (1:1; 1:8; 2:3). Eliphaz, Bildad and Zophar later found that they were entirely wrong about this man (42:7,8).

Is it sinful to falsely accuse anyone? It is, if it is wrong to be like Satan; for he is the original and continual false accuser. It is as wrong as abomination: "He that justifieth the wicked, and he that condemneth the just, even they both are abomination to the Lord" (Prov. 17:15).

Christ many times suffered the sting of false accusations. Some called him a blasphemer (Jno. 10:33). They stated it, but this did not make it so. "Consider him that endureth such contradiction of sinners against himself" (Heb. 12:3). He was crucified upon the testimony of false witnesses (Matt. 26: 60,61). At times he explained his conduct to his accusers, but most often he said nothing. At times a defense is in order. Most often, however, a defense is useless. Real friends do not need an explanation. Enemies will accept none.

Christ's followers sometimes experience the same heartache, and nothing tests one's character more than having something evil said about him (Matt. 5:11). Some people are turned aside from the grandeur of their life-work by so pursuing personal grievances that their lives become no more than a petty warfare with their enemies. David refused to do this. When Shemei cursed him, he said: "Let him curse... it may be... that the Lord will requite me good for his cursing this day." He believed that the Lord had the power to turn his enemies' darts into blessings along the way.

ALL OTHER FRIENDS FORSOOK JOB

Nobody would be surprised to see evil men forsake evil men, but we would expect good men to stand by good men. Do they? Seldom. Job had befriended many. When his trials came, many should have been anxious to return the favor. The record tells of only four who cared enough to try. It seems that all others were like shadows — close by on sunny days but nowhere to be found on cloudy days: "My kinsfolk have failed me, and my familiar friends have forgotten me... All my inward friends abhorred me: and they whom I loved are turned against me" (19:14-19). One who seems to be a good friend today may be an enemy tomorrow. Why?

Some turn away when wealth is gone. "Wealth maketh many friends" (Prov. 19:4). "The rich hath many friends" (Prov. 14:20). Evidently many had gathered around Job because of his riches and prominence. They liked the feasting and gaiety, belonging to the "in" crowd. When his wealth was gone, why waste more time with him? Many followed Christ only for the loaves and fishes (Jno. 6:26).

Some forsake friends because of a lack of courage. Eliphaz, Bildad and Zophar expressed the common view of the day — that suffering was a sign of sin — so evidently most of Job's acquaintances shared this view. Can't you just hear the tongues that must have wagged over the city with such "juicy tidbits" as: "Have you heard about Job? What in the world has he done to deserve such punishment? I really wouldn't have thought it of him." Most people would not want to be classed as his friend, fearing to bring reproach upon themselves, unwilling to go against public opinion. When the sentiment of the people turned against Christ, even his beloved friend Peter did not want to be counted among his friends (Matt. 26:69-75). He simply did not have enough courage to do so.

UNJUSTLY USED AS AN OBJECT OF SHAME AND CONTEMPT

Notice the treatment Job received: "Yea, young children despised me: I arose, and they spake against me" (19:18). "I am their byword. They abhor me, they flee far from me, and spare not to spit in my face" (30:9,10). He had become the laughing-stock of the whole city (12:4). Such ignominious treatment would not have been accorded a man merely for physical illness. Why then?

Because he was erroneously regarded as a wicked man. Evidently some welcomed a chance to heap contempt upon him, for it made them feel whiter and more righteous by comparison.

Because he was a spiritual giant among men, and the world has always had its little men who love to be giant-killers. Envy consumes them, and their greatest sense of triumph comes from sniping at, wounding and trying to destroy their superiors. No doubt some gloated over an opportunity to knock the giant Job down from his pinnacle of honor and to join the parade of self-righteous spiritual pygmies that trampled him deeper into the dust of despair.

Christ unjustly suffered the same heartache. "They did spit in his face, and buffeted him; and others smote him with the palm of their hands" (Matt. 26:67). Why? What had he done to deserve such treatment? Nothing, but he had been charged as a sinner. It was popular to be against him, rather than for him. He, too, was a spiritual giant, the greatest among men—and envious little people put the giant to death (Matt. 27:18).

This is one of the bitterest of all trials. Physical pain, as terrible as it is, is not the worst kind of suffering. A broken heart is infinitely harder to bear than a broken body. Christ "endured the cross, despising the shame" (Heb. 12:2). Any person who has endured both intense physical pain and deep wounds of the spirit will testify that it was easier for Christ to endure the cross than to despise the shame. Yes, a broken heart is worse than a broken body.

REVIEW EXERCISE

1. What was Mrs. Job's suggestion to her husband? ....

....

2. What was Satan trying to get Job to do? ....

3. What was Job's answer to his wife? ....

....

4. How do we know that the friends' accusations of Job were false?

....

5. He that condemns the just is an .... to the Lord.

Scripture: ....

6. Of what was Christ falsely accused? ....

7. "Wealth maketh ...."

8. What caused Peter to fail to stand by Christ in his time of trial?

....

9. What kind of treatment was heaped upon Job? ....

....

....

10. With whom did the expression "skin of my teeth" originate?

....

11. What did Job say his friends used to "break me in pieces"?

....

FOR THOUGHT OR DISCUSSION

1. What about the old adage: "Where's there smoke, there's bound to be fire"? Was this true concerning Christ? There was so much smoke that he was sentenced to death. Where did the smoke originate? Did it come from the fire of truth or from the fire of falsehoods? You know. Enemies deliberately produced the smoke from lies and smears in a planned effort to destroy him.
2. Name some other Biblical characters who endured the same experience.
3. In your opinion, what was the most difficult phase of Job's testing?
4. Job's friends attempted to console but actually did more harm than good. Discuss Job's words to them (16:1-7). How do "miserable comforters" today sometimes cause more distress than comfort? In times of sickness? In times of bereavement?

V

The Tempest Inside

A perplexed and depressed man once said: "I have enough chaos on the inside of me for the Lord to make another world out of." Have you ever felt like this? Evidently Job did. The storm which descended upon him was great, but the one which raged within him was greater. In the most vivid description ever penned, his tempest-tossed spirit is pictured in all its sorrow, disappointment and befogged questionings; and in it we see our own hearts — only written in larger print. God's word speaks of others who felt the same way (Psa. 61:2; 143:4; Isa. 54:11-14).

Anguish of spirit is the acutest form of pain. "The spirit of a man will sustain his infirmity; but a wounded spirit who can bear?" (Prov. 18:14). Our major battles with the Evil One are fought within us. This is where we either win or lose. In *Gone With the Wind* one of the characters was described like this: "There warn't nuthin' from the outside world that could lick him. But he had a common failin'; he could be licked from the inside." So beware! We cannot control what happens *to us;* therefore, we must control what happens *in us.* Job can help. Look at the elements which composed the storm within him.

Loneliness

Bitter distress often seeks solitude. Job retired alone to the ash heap. Man needs at times to be alone, for solitude is a healing balm necessary for the heart's health. There is a vast difference, however, between solitude and loneliness. One may be alone and not be lonely. On the other hand, one may be lonely in the midst of many people. Job had been forsaken by family and friends. This is hard enough to bear, but the height of his loneliness came when he felt that the Lord had forsaken him (23:3-9). *Loneliness breeds despair.* Shelley wrote:

> Then Black Despair
> The shadow of a starless night, was thrown
> Over the world in which I moved alone.

The climax of Christ's trials came on the cross when, as the sins of the world were laid upon him, God turned from him — for he cannot countenance sin. The anguished spirit cried: "My God, my God, why hast thou forsaken me?" (Matt. 27:46). He reached the pinnacle of loneliness, though others stood by. If hell were nothing more than being separated from God, it would still be hell. A bare foretaste of this horror has been experienced by such men as Thomas Paine, renowned infidel, who is said to have exclaimed on his deathbed:

> I would give worlds, if I had them, if *The Age of Reason* had never been published. O Lord help me! Christ, help me! Stay with me! It is hell to be left alone.

Doctors testify that loneliness is one of the most prevalent heartaches. However, if the Lord is with us, we are never alone, though the whole world should forsake us. This was true of Job, though he did not realize it.

THE GRIEF THAT DEATH BRINGS

Sorrow was compounded in the lonely man's heart by the loss of every child at once. If you have traveled the path of anguish to the silent city of the dead and laid to rest the body of one you brought into the world, then you can begin to understand the shattering grief of the devoted father. Everyone who has stood beside the still form of a beloved can feel every tear-stained word of his agonizing cry: "O that my grief were thoroughly weighed, and my calamity laid in the balances together! For now it would be heavier than the sand of the sea" (6:2,3).

Human ties can be so close and precious, for our ability to love is a part of our kinship with the Divine. God is love. When there is a union of the spirit binding hearts together, they are inseparable. The loss of such a dear one severs a part of our being which can never be replaced. When we realize that never, never, never again will we feel the touch of a loved one's hand or hear the sound of a voice so cherished and comforting, the despair is all-consuming. The world is filled with those who sit alone beside an empty chair and bathe the heart's ever-present wound with the balm of tears. The only real comfort must come from memory and hope—memory of all the beautiful and strengthening associations, and hope of being reunited with those so dear. Christians have this comfort (I Thess. 4:13-18). Job lived before these reassuring words were written, but he reasoned that it was the Lord who had been good enough to give him precious sons and daughters for awhile (1:20,21). Misfortune can take away only that which good fortune gave.

PROLONGED SLEEPLESSNESS AND INTENSE WEARINESS

The blessing of sleep can be realized only by those who have experienced prolonged sleeplessness. Job knew. "When I lie down, I say, When shall I arise, and the night be gone? I am full of tossings to and fro unto the dawning of the day" (7:4). His fitful moments of rest were plagued by horrible nightmares: "When I say, My bed shall comfort me, my couch shall ease my complaint; then thou scarest me with dreams, and terrifiest me through visions" (7:13,14).

Problems are always intensified at night. Things bearable

by day can seem overwhelmingly burdensome at night. Why? The sights and sounds and obligations of the day often keep our minds diverted. When darkness shuts those out and quietness fills the house, full attention is turned inward. One is thrown directly upon the resources of his own soul, brought face to face with himself and with God.

In time almost everyone experiences sleepless hours, either because of physical pain or other difficulties. This time of introspection can be beneficial, an opportunity for self-examination and quiet communion with God, through prayer and recalling His words in the darkness and calm of night. A sweet elderly lady says that, rather than counting sheep, she counts God's promises to her, going over their comforting assurances one by one.

Physical fatigue and illness always accentuate our problems. Weariness of body increases weariness of spirit, and vice versa. Because of pain and sleeplessness, Job could get relief from neither. He said: "My soul is weary of my life" (10:1). As the tired laborer longs for eventide, the over-burdened heart longs for rest. Shelley expressed it so vividly:

> I could lie down like a tired child
> And weep away this life of care
> Which I have borne and still must bear.

THE PAIN AND COMFORT OF MEMORY

Memory is a gift of God. It can be both intensely painful and wonderfully comforting. Job recalled the glorious yesterdays filled with honor, prosperity and happiness (29:2-25). The memory at once blessed and pained him as he contrasted the past with his present wretchedness (30:1,9,10).

Some days are so distressing that our only comfort must come from the memory of past joys, which can never be taken from us, and from the hope of future bliss promised the faithful. Sweet memories can be a treasure house of joys stored up for the day of despair, to be taken out and examined again lovingly and gratefully one by one when the day seems to furnish no treasure of its own.

> **Bliss in possession will not last;**
> **Remembered joys are never past;**
> **At once the fountain, stream, and sea,**
> **They were, they are, they yet shall be.**
> **— James Montgomery**

DISAPPOINTMENT IN FRIENDS AND LOVED ONES

Have you ever been so disappointed in a beloved one that you were left reeling in stunned disbelief? This is one of the sharpest pains that can pierce the human heart. It can wound deeper than death and send one to the pit of despondency. When Job's lifetime companion and dear friends forsook him, no doubt he asked himself over and over: "Is it really true?" If he had not experienced it, he never could have believed it.

Think of the deep wound of Christ's heart when Judas, a close friend, betrayed him into enemy hands. This was prophesied: "All that hate me whisper together against me: against me do they devise my hurt... Yea, mine own familiar friend, in whom I trusted, which did eat of my bread, hath lifted up his heel against me" (Psa. 41:7-9). Surely David, who penned this prophecy, could understand the feeling described, for he had experienced the same heartache. His beloved son Absalom led an army against him — which was not just the revolt of a son against his father but also rebellion against God, for David was God's anointed. To see a son fall below the high standard once instilled in him is a grief greater than death. This realization intensified his sorrow when news came of the rebellious son's death. From the anguished father came one of the most heart-rending cries ever penned: "O my son

Absalom, my son, my son Absalom! would God I had died for thee, O Absalom, my son, my son!" (II Sam. 18:33).

A FEELING OF WORTHLESSNESS

"My life is wind," Job said (7:7). He felt worthless to himself and everyone else. Disease had rendered him incapable of any useful endeavor. All that was left of him was an emaciated body, scarcely more than a mass of repulsive eruptions stretched over pain-racked bones, in which dwelt a tormented and restless spirit. So what good was life? He could see no purpose in it.

However, no person is capable of judging the worth of his own life. If Job had known that he was casting a giant shadow to be seen through the centuries, he could have taken heart. When you are engulfed in problems which seem too great to bear, take courage. You do not know how much your victory may encourage others who watch from a distance. What may seem worthless to you may serve to stabilize another's tottering steps and turn him from failure to success.

OVERWHELMING DESPAIR

All these things combined to produce complete despair in Job's heart. Yes, even the strongest bend momentarily under pressure. His extreme depression was not merely the product of a discontented mind, nor was it the hasty judgment of an impatient man. His words of anguish were wrung from him only after the most terrible combination of circumstances and after much deliberation. He had thought for at least seven days, and probably much longer, before ever saying a word. He had carefully weighed his condition. As he did, he sank deeper and deeper into the throes of despondency.

WEEPING, WEEPING, WEEPING

"My face is foul with weeping, and on my eyelids is the

shadow of death," said the suffering, discouraged man (16:16). He was not a weakling. He was a brave man with immense strength and character, but there is a time for tears. The ability to weep is a God-given blessing. When the heart is filled with so much emotion that it almost bursts, tears are the safety-valves. That was about the only therapy available to Job, and thus his befogged spirit sought relief with tears, tears — *tears which rained down from the tempest raging within him.*

A DESIRE FOR DEATH

Despair can reach such depths that one is left with no desire to live. Job had rejected his wife's suggestion of self-destruction, but he longed for death "more than for hid treasures" (3:21; 6:8,9). "So my soul chooseth strangling and death rather than my life. I loathe it" (7:15). He was not the first or the last to reach this low level of despondency. Jeremiah wished he had never been born (Jer. 20:14-18), and Elijah asked the Lord to take his life (I Ki. 19:4).

There is a picture in a gallery in Italy which portrays death coming into the midst of a group of people. The young, the strong, the gay flee from it in terror. The sick, the suffering, the aged and the weary reach forth arms of welcome. However, despair afflicts not only the aged and the sick but has become in our time a major problem among the young. Among college-age young people suicide is the second most prevalent cause of death, exceeded only by automobile accidents. In such cases, the tempest raging within them became too violent to handle and they, like Job, longed for the quietness of the grave: "Where the wicked cease from troubling, and there the weary be at rest" (3:17). However, we must all realize that the grave brings no rest to the unfaithful or disobedient. Our lives are sacred. Though Job and Elijah and Jeremiah hit such depths that they lost their desire to live, they steadfastly refused to take the matter into their own hands. Such would have been wrong (I Cor. 3:17).

Though Job asked for death, he actually longed for life, a more transcendent life. This is fully confirmed by his statements of faith and hope.

> **Whatever crazy Sorrow saith**
> **No life that breathes with human breath**
> **Hath ever truly longed for death.**
> **'Tis life whereof our nerves are scant;**
> **Oh, life, not death for which we pant;**
> **More life and fuller life we want.**

HOPELESSNESS AND HOPE, DOUBT AND FAITH

Despair is a mixture of emotions, strangely inconsistent. Contradictory forces tug at the heart, clearly evident in the spirit of our hero. Hopelessness beset him: "My days are... spent without hope" (7:6,7). In hopelessness one always searches for a ray of light, something to dispel the terrible darkness. When he thinks he has found it, he seizes upon it and tries to hold on, only at times to lose his grip and sink back into the darkness. This happened to Job. Yet it was the agony of hopelessness which led him to hope. How can this be? Finding no relief in this world, he turned his attention to the next world. Hopelessness for the outer man strengthened his hope for the inner man (II Cor. 4:16-18). It can do the same for us.

Questionings and doubts beset him, and he often switched from bewildered melancholy to heights of optimism, strength and courage. It is as though he would say to himself: "Many things I cannot understand, but this one thing I know."

Yes, despair is like this — filled with inconsistences. It vacillates between light and darkness, ups and downs, hope and hopelessness, faith and doubt. In time one must take precedence over the other. In Chapter X we shall consider our triumph over despair.

REVIEW EXERCISE

1. How did Job describe the weight of his grief? ....

....

2. What kind of miseries did Job experience at night? ....

....

....

3. Name some of the wonderful joys of Job's past which he recalled.

....

....

4. Who "lifted up his heel" against Christ? ....

5. Job said, "My face is foul with ...."

6. He described the grave as a place "where the ....

   cease from ...."

   Note that it does not say they cease from trouble. Their trouble is just beginning, but rather they cease from troubling or harming others. The wicked trouble this earth, but the time will come when they can no longer do so.

7. Where did Job say he had looked for God? ....

....

8. What words of loneliness did Christ utter on the cross? ....

....

9. (T or F) It would be wrong to destroy our bodies.

   Scripture: ....

FOR THOUGHT OR DISCUSSION

1. Tears can signify many things, for what makes a person weep

is one index to his whole being. It can be either a sign of strength or weakness. Esau wept over his lost heritage. Israel wept for the fleshpots of Egypt. Delilah wept to get her selfish way with Samson. Hezekiah wept because he was about to die. Peter wept with repentance. Mary and Martha wept with grief. Christ wept with concern over lost souls.

2. Despair often blinds one, for that which causes the present distress can loom so large in the mind that one's vision is completely obscured and he cannot see his many blessings and comforts.

3. Though Elijah said he no longer desired to live, did he really want to die? If so, why did he flee from Jezebel? Despair often provokes rash statements.

4. If you have ever lost a child, discuss the words of Job at that time (1:20,21). How much spiritual strength is required to maintain this attitude?

VI

"I Am Full of Confusion"

NOTHING disturbs one's peace of mind more than spiritual doubts. Satan knows this, and one of his ingenious tricks is to get men to doubt. By it he can break the faith link which binds one to the Father. This accounts for much of the unrest today. One who is unsure about God, about eternity, about his own soul, has no anchor. Therefore, he is mercilessly tossed upon life's stormy sea and filled with confusion.

> **O, how this tyrant, doubt, torments my breast!**
> **My thoughts, like birds, who, frighten'd from their nest,**
> **Around the place where all was hush'd before,**
> **Flutter, and hardly nestle any more.**
>
> **— Otway**

This was a part of the tempest which raged within Job. So many unanswered questions flooded his mind concerning the nature of man, life, death, eternity and God's justice. His perplexity reached a climax with these words: "I am full of confusion" (10:15). The questions which confused him still challenge our thinking today just as strongly as ever. The only difference is that the fulness of divine revelation has given us additional light. He asked: "What is man?" "If a man die, shall he live again?" "Where shall wisdom be found?" "Why do the wicked prosper?" "How can a man be just with God?"

"What Is Man?" (7:17)

Job could not understand why he, a mere man, should be the object of such intense affliction. "What is man . . . that thou shouldst visit him every morning and try him every moment?" (7:17,18). It implies man's insignificance, but considering the question verifies man's worth in God's sight. Amid all the complexities and enormities of the universe, he was mindful of this one lone life.

What is man? Philosophers through the ages have wrestled with this question. David did (Psa. 8:4). So has every thoughtful person. What one believes about man — his origin, his nature, his destiny — will determine his whole life here and hereafter. Therefore, no question is more practical or pertinent to our eternal welfare. This is your question and mine, just as surely as it was Job's. What is man?

Man is a creature with spiritual capacities, made in the image of God. Only man has a conscience, a sense of right and wrong, the ability to contemplate the eternal, to see the invisible and to possess qualities of the spirit such as faith, hope, patience and godliness.

Man, therefore, is a dual being, more than flesh. He is an immortal spirit (II Cor. 4:16-18).

Man is a creature with amazing mental capabilities—a mind which enables him to dominate the universe, to possess reason, knowledge, memory, judgment and foresight. Only man seeks to improve himself and his surroundings. He thinks and plans and strives to build a better life. He can erect skyscrapers, throw his voice around the world, and explore outer space — yet he cannot direct his own steps. (Jer. 10:23,24).

Man is the crowning work of all God's creation, and yet the only object of his regret (Gen. 6:6).

Man is an "epistle . . . known and read of all men" (II Cor. 3:2) — therefore, a creature of vast and far-reaching influence. Job could not realize that his life was an epistle to be read by millions, but it was.

Man is a creature whose intrinsic value is about one dollar — yet he is *worth more than all the combined wealth of the world* (Matt. 8:36,37).

Man's value is seen in the price God was willing to pay for his redemption: his only Son (Rom. 5:8). This Scripture shows the purchaser, the price and the person redeemed. Not until then was Job's question fully answered. What is man? Not an object of vengeance but an object of the unspeakable love and concern of a heavenly Father.

"IF A MAN DIE, SHALL HE LIVE AGAIN?" (14:14).

Since Job saw no hope of better days in this world, his mind naturally turned to the question: "What after this life?" "Shall we live again?" He discussed the question and reasoned that:

The testimony of experience seemed to be against it. He had observed that a tree may be cut down, and it will sprout again (14:7-9); but he had never seen a man rise again after he had been laid in the grave (14:14).

Yet, the phenomenon of nature suggests a resurrection. The very fact that the tree sprouts again is testimony of a Power greater than all nature. Man, in all his ingenuity, cannot make a tree sprout. Yet there is a Force which resurrects all things of nature each spring. Would such a Being allow man to remain forever in the dust? It would be unreasonable.

The nature of man demands a resurrection. Though Job longed for rest and quietude of the grave, he did not want to remain there forever. He did not desire annihilation. He wanted the Father to remember him and call him forth: "O that thou wouldest hide me in the grave, that thou wouldest keep me secret, until thy wrath be past, that thou wouldest appoint me a set time, and remember me!" (14:13).

If there is no resurrection, we are of all creatures most pitiable. Disease, disability, death and dust! Is this all we have to look forward to? Yes, if there should be no resurrection! The very thought causes our hearts to sink. Then we can say "Amen" to Paul's statement: "If in this life only we have hope in Christ, we are of all men most miserable" (I Cor. 15:19).

The nature of God demands a resurrection. "Thou shalt call, and I will answer thee: thou wilt have a desire to the work of thine hands" (14:15). It is utterly inconceivable that the Creator would allow man, whom he fashioned with his own hands and stamped with his own image, to lie forever forgotten in the dust. Job reasoned that since he had such a longing to see his heavenly Father, to talk with him and be with him, would not the Father also have a desire to be reunited with his own handiwork? What loving father can suffocate a desire to see his offspring? Therefore, the perplexed man felt that surely: "Thou shalt call, and I will answer thee."

Job reached his conclusion, after all his thinking and reasoning: "And after my skin, even this body is destroyed, then without my flesh shall I see God" (19:26, A.S.V.). Yes, he fully believed that he would live again.

The testimony of revelation confirms a resurrection. David spoke of a life after death (Psa. 16:11). So did Isaiah (Isa. 26:19), Daniel (Dan. 12:2) and others. It was not until Christ came, however, that it was fully preached (Jno. 5:28, 29).

Christ proved the resurrection. "But now is Christ risen from the dead and become the firstfruits of them that sleep" (I Cor. 15:20). The resurrection of Christ is a certain event of history — so much so that even Josephus, who never became a Christian, declared it to be an accepted fact of his day.

"If a man die, shall he live again?" Yes. Christ answered Job's question conclusively, and again revelation confirmed it (I Thess. 4:13-18). "Comfort one another with these words."

"BUT WHERE SHALL WISDOM BE FOUND?" (28:12)

As all of us, Job wondered about wisdom, and in an interesting and enlightening discussion states his conclusions. In our age of intellectualism, many and varied are the voices that presume to define wisdom. Who is wise? Is there a standard of wisdom?

Man must learn the source of wisdom. If you want to find something, you must look in the right place. You can never find it by looking in a place where it is not. Job observed that men know where to find silver, gold, iron and brass (28: 1,2). Bread comes from the earth (28:5). But where would you go to get wisdom?

It does not originate with men (28:21).

It cannot be bought with money (28:15). You can't go to a store — or even to a university — and buy it, even with billions; yet its value is far beyond any priceless jewel (28:16-19). Then where can you find wisdom?

God only "knoweth the place thereof" (28:23). It is his secret alone, the Absolute Source of wisdom. Therefore, man must go to the Source. How? By studying nature? Though divine wisdom is surely manifest in nature, this is not the whole of it. Though all of nature is of God, all of nature is not all of God. We must look further. God's revealed wisdom is his Word. Job thus concluded: "Behold, the fear of the Lord, that is wisdom; and to depart from evil is understanding" (28:28). Without the revealed Word, man could not know the Father's will or how to depart from evil.

An intellectually honest person is forced to an acceptance of God and his superior knowledge in all areas of thought and endeavor. Why? When man exercises his full intellectual capacities, he realizes there is so much more beyond his reach. This testifies of a Superior Intelligence. As an illustration, consider this simple diagram:

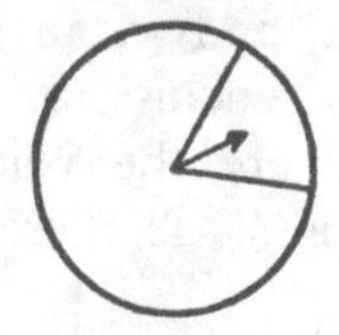

Let the circle represent all knowledge. Let the dot in the center represent man as he launches out to increase his knowledge in any particular field.

For example, consider medical science. Men have made outstanding discoveries. Yet as their scope of knowledge increases, they see more clearly than ever their own limitations and ignorance, the vast unknown realm before them.

This forcefully testifies of a Superior Intelligence. Knowledge which is yet to be obtained by man already belongs to Someone. Knowledge which man now possesses has belonged to Someone all the time. Man has merely discovered that which was set in order long ago by Someone other than man.

An intellectually honest person will be led to humility, not conceit, as his knowledge increases. The wisest, best informed, and greatest people are very humble. Why? Because the further one travels into the realm of knowledge, the more clearly he sees how much more is yet to be learned. Then he freely admits that his ignorance exceeds his knowledge. This fosters humility.

This is true in every field of thought and endeavor. The truly great people are humble. Therefore, one who is proud and puffed up, thinking that he knows nearly everything, is but broadcasting the fact that he has not yet traveled very far out into the sea of knowledge. This is a lesson much needed by young and old alike today. Even if one should master all knowledge possible in any one field, think of the many other areas in which he is relatively ignorant. Then, there is no place for pride or arrogance for any human being.

George Washington Carver was one of the most outstanding scientists this nation has produced. His intellectual brilliance was accompanied by simplicity, humility and faith in God. Those who knew him well relate that he often took students on field trips. He would explain some wonder of nature and then comment: "I want you to keep in mind that this is God's work, and there is still so much that we don't know about it."

An engineer said: "The most brilliant engineer I know is a very humble man, easy to talk with about any problem. So many respect his knowledge and come to him for advice. He will listen attentively, weigh all the facts at his command, and then give an answer as simply and directly as possible." Truly, humility and simplicity are marks of wisdom and greatness.

The Bible is a book on the science of right living. God gives us all we need for an abundant life here and hereafter (Jno. 10:10). His word is truth (Jno. 17:17). It is all wisdom in matters pertaining to the spirit. Any philosophy which contradicts it is false, unwise and unworkable. Human philosophers who try to figure out all the problems of life and death apart from God and his word are like a man trapped in a pitch-dark cellar, spending his life searching for a window that isn't there — while all the time the lock is on the inside of the door. At any moment, he could unlock it and burst out into the sunlight again, but he either fails to see or refuses to admit that the door is there. He has not learned what Job knew centuries ago: "Behold, the fear of the Lord, that is wisdom: and to depart from evil is understanding." Simple! Isn't it?

REVIEW EXERCISE

1. Quote Romans 5:8 ....

....

What prompted God to send his Son? ....

2. (T or F) Job desired to remain forever in the grave.
3. What example of nature came to Job's mind as he thought about the possibility of a resurrection? ....
4. Job felt assured that "thou shall ...., and I will .... thee."
5. "................................ that are in the graves shall hear his voice, and come forth." Scripture: ....
6. "The .... of the Lord, that is wisdom; and to depart from .... is understanding."
7. (T or F) It is possible to know all about God by studying nature.
8. Name some of the many qualities possessed only by mankind, and not by animals. ....

....

....

9. Which Scripture speaks of an "outward man" and "inward man"?

....

10. In Christ's prayer to God, he said: "Thy word is ...."

Scripture: ....

FOR THOUGHT OR DISCUSSION

1. Christ was the wisest and the greatest. He taught the most profound truths the human mind is capable of grasping; yet he did so in language so simple that the common people heard him gladly. Contrast this with much of the pseudo-intellectualism of our day.
2. Job longed for some third party to intercede for him before God (9:32-35). How do Christians enjoy this privilege today?
3. What did he want to tell God? (10:2-15). He understood that his Creator knew all about him and would therefore be aware of any sin within him. Discuss his description of his own creation (10:8-12).

VII

Is God Fair?

A weary woman sat fingering her coffee cup and talking, half-way to herself and half-way to her friend across the table: "I just can't understand it. My next door neighbors never go to church and make no effort to do right. They spend most Sundays on the lake. Yet they have so much more than we do. My husband and I have spent our lives trying to serve God; but he works two jobs and I must work also just to feed our children. I have never blamed God for it, but I just wish I could understand some things better."

Evidently this is the way Job felt centuries ago. Calamities overtook him, not while he was reveling in sin, but while he was serving the Lord. This shook him so completely that he wondered if his Maker really "plays fair" with man. He had tried, but he didn't seem to be getting much consideration in return.

Why Do the Wicked Prosper?

This has always bothered God's children. Our sense of justice leads us to believe that goodness should be accompanied by comfort, and that evil should be accompanied by discomfort. Therefore, righteous men have always wondered why the Father would allow sinners to enjoy so many blessings. The question bothered Jeremiah (Jer. 12:1,2), and Habakkuk (Hab. 1:13) and Malachi (Mal. 3:13-15). It so perplexed the Psalmist that he almost lost his faith: "My feet were almost gone; my steps had well nigh slipped" (Psa. 73:2).

Job was so puzzled over the prosperity and ease of evil men

in contrast with his own hardships. He asked: "Wherefore do the wicked live, become old, yea, are mighty in power?" (21:7). The problem returned to his mind time after time (12:6; 21:7-30; 24:2-25; 27:8-23). He observed that evildoers completely spurned God and yet seemed to live joyfully; their houses were safe; they wielded great power on earth, enjoyed feasting and gaiety and immense wealth; and then death came suddenly without the lingering miseries he was experiencing. It just didn't seem fair. This aspect of human affairs and an effort to unravel it is a major point in his debate. From his reasoning he finally reached some very sound conclusions which can be most helpful to all righteous people, both young and old.

Why does the Lord allow sinners to prosper? We cannot know all the answers, but some basic principles are evident from his Word.

The prosperity of the wicked confirms the need of a future judgment and thus forcefully argues in favor of immortality. We have a sense of justice and believe in justice. Yet, if there is no life beyond this one, there is no such thing as justice — for it is not found in this world. The righteous, the innocent, the deserving are often mistreated, while the unrighteous go unpunished. Not because our Father is unjust, but because of the presence of Satan and sin in the world. Justice demands a fair accounting some day. Job concluded this (21:30; 27:22). Therefore, we must look beyond this world for the answers to this question. Those who attempt to solve all humanity's problems with a this-world-only philosophy are baffled, for they encounter insurmountable difficulties. This is one question to which they have no answer at all.

The prosperity of the wicked verifies the dependability of the Creator's physical and economic laws. He set them in order for man's well-being, and those who abide by them will be blessed materially. He sends rain on the just and the unjust (Matt. 5:45). The non-Christian farmer, banker, merchant or lawyer will profit economically, if he follows God's economic laws. To be blessed spiritually, however, one must obey God's spiritual laws.

The prosperity of the wicked testifies of the heavenly Father's merciful forbearance in hope of their repentance. The punishment of the wicked is delayed for reasons sometimes not apparent to us; but in this we can see the longsuffering love and patience of God. His goodness to them, even while in their sins, has motivated many to renounce Satan and turn to the Father (Rom. 2:4). Suppose this one should be your son or daughter, how much patience would you want the Father to manifest toward an evildoer?

The prosperity of the wicked serves to test the faith of the righteous. If ever a man could be tempted to turn away from God because of seeming injustices, it was Job. That was a part of his test. Though the question mystified him, he refused to let it destroy his faith. He thought and thought about the matter in the light of his own acute problems. He could readily see that prosperity is no sign of divine approval (12:6). Therefore, he completely rejected his friends' philosophy that suffering indicates sin (21:34) and concluded that adversity is no sign of divine disapproval. One's status before God cannot be gauged by earthly ease or prosperity, disease or adversity. The success of the wicked does test the faith of the righteous, for God warns: "Fret not thyself because of evildoers, neither be thou envious" (Psa. 37:1).

"Fret not thyself." Fret not because of evil done to you — whether some discourtesy, ingratitude, mistreatment or persecution. The evildoer, not you, must account for it — so fret not. "Fret not thyself" because of some sinner's success.

"Neither be thou envious." If we understood the condition

of the wicked, surely there would be no cause for envy, for we certainly would not want to exchange places with them. Why? Consider further some of Job's conclusions:

(1) The joys of the wicked are fleeting; they will soon pass away (21:18; 24:24; Psa. 37:2,13). Their only rewards are being enjoyed now (Matt. 6:2,5,16).

(2) Trouble will come to them, even in this life. Then their possessions cannot feed their souls or comfort their hearts. Then they will need God but will not have access to him (27:8-10; Jno. 9:31). "If God be for us, who can be against us?" And if God be against us, what does it matter who is for us? It avails nothing.

(3) Their ease is superficial, for they are plagued by deep-seated fears. Some day terrors will consume them, for they are living in "slippery places" (27:20; Psa. 73:18,19).

(4) Eternal destruction awaits evildoers (21:30; 27:22; Matt 25:30,46). Job realized this. All of these considerations caused him to resolve: "My righteousness I hold fast, and will not let it go; my heart shall not reproach me so long as I live" (27:6).

Therefore, "neither be thou envious." No matter how great may be sinners' prosperity, popularity, prestige, power or pleasure — envy them not. You would not want to trade places with them. The Psalmist decided he had been very foolish to let such a problem upset him (Psa. 73:22). How vain and empty is a little earthly success when compared with all the comforts and joys of the godly, both here and hereafter (Psa. 73:23-28; 37:3-11).

CHARGING GOD FOOLISHLY

"In all this Job sinned not, nor charged God foolishly" (1:22). Some men have foolishly accused the Father of being unfair and thus rebelled against him — not only because of the prosperity of the wicked, but note other reasons:

Some have accused God of injustice because of mass destruction, such as the cities of Sodom and Gomorrah, declaring it to be unfair to take the lives of the innocent along with the guilty (Gen. 19:24,25). Man is prone to put too much emphasis upon this life, while God sees the eternal. Think for a moment. In these cities three classes of people were destroyed: (1) The wicked. Our sense of justice permits us to understand their destruction. (2) The righteous. Would they actually be better off to go on to heaven? Paul thought so (Phil. 1:23). Thus, death was no injustice to them. (3) The innocent babies and children. Would God be doing them a favor or disfavor by taking them on to heaven, rather than allowing them to grow up in the midst of great wickedness and risk losing their souls?

Some have charged God with unfairness because of man's sins. Wars are the result of man's sins. Somebody has done wrong or there would never be a war. Yet grief and anguish have caused some to cry out in rebellion: "God is unjust, or he would not allow wars." A young mother deserted her husband and two children. In his shock and sorrow, the young man concluded: "God is cruel, or he would not let this happen to me." He was blaming the Lord for giving his wife individual freedom; but if she had not been given it, she could not have married him in the first place. We must not foolishly charge God with man's sins.

The death of a loved one has caused some to accuse God of injustice. In the first place, death is sometimes the result of man's mistakes, as discussed in Chapter XI. In the next place, the Father has appointed death not to harm but to bless his children. These bodies are not suited to an eternal existence (I Cor. 15:50). Death is the doorway to the realm where

"God shall wipe away all tears from their eyes, and there shall be no more death, neither sorrow, nor crying, neither shall there be any more pain" (Rev. 21:4). No wonder Paul says it is gain for the righteous (Phil. 1:21) — a thing precious in the sight of Jehovah (Psa. 116:15).

Others have questioned God's justice because of physical handicaps suffered by the innocent. For instance, some have asked: "Why should one be born blind and endure this hardship for a lifetime through no fault of his own? It seems so unfair." We can never know all the answers, but we can know for sure that it is not a result of God's injustice. Our perplexity stems from our human view of things, which is necessarily a partial view. What is good? What is bad? What is fortune? What is misfortune? We are inclined to define prosperity and ease as good, and to define pain and adversity as bad; but this is not necessarily true. It would be far wiser and more accurate to use the following definitions: *anything which draws one closer to God is good; anything which leads one further away from God is bad.* This will produce an altogether different concept of life. What person among us is prepared to judge whether a supposed handicap is a blessing or a curse? Even if we did not consider the spiritual aspect at all, some of the world's most outstanding accomplishments have been achieved in adverse circumstances.

For instance, Arturo Toscanini was so near-sighted that he grew weary of having to bend close to his musical score sheet. He decided to memorize all his music. He did so, not only for his cello but for every part in the orchestra. When he was only nineteen years of age, one night in an opera house in Italy, as the orchestra was scheduled to begin, word came that the conductor was very ill. Toscanini was asked to conduct. He closed the score book and conducted the entire opera from memory. He received a mighty ovation and was later made the permanent conductor. His physical handicap proved to be a blessing by which he climbed to the top in his field.

If Milton had not lost his sight, it is entirely possible that the world would have known little of him. He attained such literary heights that someone has defined poetry as that which Milton saw after he became blind. Who can say his blindness was misfortune?

Fanny J. Crosby's blindness caused her to develop talents which probably would otherwise have remained dormant. It forced a contemplation of life's invisible values which she expressed in approximately six thousand poems and hymns which have elevated and comforted millions. She could have sat in the corner and drawn the cloak of self-pity around her. Instead, she recognized soon in life that her seeming handicap was actually her greatest blessing. This was her attitude:

> Oh, what a happy soul am I!
> Although I cannot see,
> I am resolved that in this world
> Contented I will be;
> How many blessings I enjoy
> That other people don't!
> To weep and sigh because I'm blind
> I cannot, and I won't.

So no person should ever use physical hardships to question divine justice. Rather — let us be careful lest we charge God foolishly.

REVIEW EXERCISE

1. List some of the descriptive terms used concerning the wicked in Psa. 73:2-12. ....

....

....

2. What helped to give the Psalmist a better understanding of this

problem? (Psa. 73:17). ....

....

3. What figures of speech did Job use to describe the temporary and fleeting prosperity of the wicked? ....

....

4. (T or F) God will not answer the requests of the wicked who call upon him.

5. Job concluded that .... would be the eternal fate of the unrighteous.

6. (T or F) Realizing God's goodness toward them, even while in their sins, should lead evildoers to repentance. Scripture ....

....

7. What is actually good fortune? ....

....

What is really misfortune? ....

....

8. Give some of the things which have caused man to foolishly charge God. ....

....

....

9. Considering the fate of the wicked caused Job to resolve: "My .... I hold fast, and will not let it go; my .... shall not reproach me so long as I live."

FOR THOUGHT OR DISCUSSION

1. We have often heard that many misfortunes may actually be blessings in disguise, and this is certainly taught in God's word. We are reminded of the man who quipped: "I have had so many blessings in disguise lately that I would surely like to have a few which are not quite so disguised!"
2. It is relatively easy to "fret not thyself because of evildoers," if the evil is done to someone else. How easy is it when the evil is done to you?
3. How can the following things be either good or bad, fortune or misfortune? Health? Wealth? Popularity? Physical beauty? Profession? Friends?

VIII

Words Without Knowledge

HAVE you ever felt that you just had to say something, or else burst? If so, you are not the first one. The Bible speaks of more than one. Jeremiah once felt as though he had a fire inside him. He had resolved no longer to try to teach rebellious people, but the word of God burned within him so that he could stand it no longer. He had to speak (Jer. 20:9).

Elihu, a young man, had listened silently and intently to the prolonged debate between Job and his three friends. Finally, he could stand it no longer. He said he was about to burst like a bottle filled with new wine (32:19). He had to speak.

Conviction Compelled the Young Man

Elihu explained why he had not spoken previously: "I am young, and ye are very old . . . I said, Days should speak, and multitude of years should teach wisdom" (32:6,7). He respected age and the wisdom that should accompany it. He thought years would give wisdom; therefore, he had been silent and listened to their words.

This is indeed a commendable trait. It is admirable to see a young person who is respectful of age and of wisdom, realizing that he has much yet to learn.

However, there is "a time to keep silence, and a time to speak" (Eccl. 3:7). Silence is sometimes golden, at other times yellow. To be silent when one should speak is cowardly. Elihu decided that he had been silent long enough. Conviction compelled him to speak.

The young man explained why he must say something. He detected error in the teaching of Eliphaz, Bildad and Zophar. Though they were among the most prominent men of their day, he refused to let this color his appraisal of their teachings (32:21,22). They were wrong about some things and had failed in their analysis (32:12). He declared that Job, too, needed further instruction on some points.

As the young man listened to the discussions he concluded: "Great men are not always wise: neither do the aged understand judgment" (32:9). Years do not always bring wisdom and good judgment. "But there is a spirit in man: and the inspiration of the Almighty giveth them understanding" (32:8). Whether young or old, man has a spirit capable of wisdom. Who then is wise? The one who listens to the Almighty. Man speaks words of wisdom or folly, depending upon whether his spirit is enlightened from on high. Some lessons can be learned only through experience. Therefore, the godly man who has spent many years proving divine promises in his own life can certainly speak words of wisdom to the young. However, a young man who listens to God's words is far wiser in his tender years than an aged person who does not, regardless of how worldly-wise or intelligent he may be. Elihu was convinced that he was speaking divine truth (33:3; 36:2,3). This gave the young man great courage and confidence in his message. Boldly he asserted: "I will answer thee."

"THE ALMIGHTY...IS EXCELLENT...IN PLENTY OF JUSTICE"

The fairness of the Father's dealings with man, both righteous and wicked, was the chief question debated by Job and his friends. Thus, Elihu dealt primarily with this subject. He presented masterful and enlightening arguments which deserve a more detailed study than our space will permit.

He contended that God is so much greater than man that

he is in no way obligated to give us a reason for what he does (33:12-14). If he did, we would be incapable of understanding it. We can no more fathom the mind of the Almighty than we can hold the ocean in the palm of our hand. We cannot comprehend him. If we could, he would be but one of us. Just as an animal cannot probe the depths of man's mind, for he is inferior in every way. Just as a child cannot always understand the superior wisdom of a parent's command.

The young man continued to reason that the Lord does at times afflict with pain even to the brink of the grave — but that such chastening is not punitive but disciplinary, as a loving Father deals with a child (33:17-30).

God is just, affirmed Elihu. He can be no other way. He "will not do wickedly, neither will the Almighty pervert judgment" (34:12). In support of this, he reasons:

(1) We can trust the Father's judgments, for he loves us enough to give us life and all things. Upon him we are wholly dependent, even for the breath of life within us; for if he were to "gather unto himself his spirit and his breath; all flesh shall perish together, and man shall turn again to dust" (34:14,15). How could we question our Provider and Protector?

It is possible for man to become so drunk with his own accomplishments that conceit causes him to forget his complete dependence upon his Creator. An interesting story appeared in the Illinois Bell Telephone news. Two reporters were on a tour of a new telephone building. As they viewed the maze of equipment, one of them was intrigued by observing a small bowl in the midst of all the ingenious mechanisms. It was filled with water, wherein two goldfish swam. "What is that for?" the curious newsman asked. "That," replied his companion, "was probably put there to remind mortals that some very wonderful things were also invented by God."

(2) God is the "most just"—the author of justice (34:17). Therefore, he will not govern unjustly. Justice demands that wickedness be punished and righteousness rewarded. Neither darkness nor death will enable workers of iniquity to escape this divine judgment (34:21-29). We can trust the Almighty to punish the wicked and to care for the righteous — even for kings and those in authority (36:6-15). Unquestionably, God is just with man! He can be no other way. Therefore, anything which may seem to be unfairness on the Father's part must be attributed to our inferior understanding.

(3) Is God just in requiring man's obedience? Job had asked: "What profit shall I have, if I be cleansed from my sin?" (35:3). Why obey God? Does it pay? Sometimes people get the idea that they deserve the Lord's congratulations for every good deed or upright thought. Elihu discussed this most forcefully. Man's obedience is not for God's benefit. Of course, the Father is pleased with his child's righteousness, as he was Job's; but we're not doing him a big favor by living right. He is neither helped by our righteousness nor hurt by our sin:

> **If thou sinnest, what doest thou against him? or if thy transgressions be multiplied, what doest thou unto him? If thou be righteous, what givest thou him? or what receiveth he of thine hand? (35:6-9).**

So why live right? For our own good. "He that sinneth against me wrongeth his own soul" (Prov. 8:36). Every divine commandment was given to help us. We are the ones who benefit, not God; so surely it pays to serve him. Though the Devil promises higher wages, he cannot pay off.

(4) The wonders of the universe testify of God's perfection in matters of judgment and justice. Elihu said: "O Job: stand still and consider the wondrous works of God" (37:14). Only the Almighty has power over the rain, clouds, lightning,

thunder or other elements of nature (36:26-37:22). "Behold, God is mighty" (36:5). "Behold, God is great" (36:26). Man has only begun to delve into the secrets of the universe, much less to fathom the Being who created it and controls it. Scripture, experience, and even the philosophies of men verify that man can never fully comprehend God. He is too great ever to be arraigned before the bar of human reason and put on trial by mere man.

This is the inevitable conclusion: "Touching the Almighty, we cannot find him out: he is excellent in power, and in judgment, and in plenty of justice: he will not afflict" (37:23). Though "we cannot find him out," we can rest assured that his excellence in justice is on a plane with his might in the natural world. So surely our Father is just and fair. He can be no other way.

CAN MAN BE JUST WITH GOD?

Can man deal justly with the Almighty? Job wondered (9:2). Bildad did not think it possible. He advanced the idea that nothing is pure in God's eyes — least of all, man — but in this he erred (25:4-6).

Man cannot be sinless and therefore cannot, through his own goodness, walk in purity. However, *he can walk acceptably before his Maker.* Job did. We can — not by morality alone or by works of the old law, but by obedience to Christ (Gal. 2:16). Then the Saviour's blood will bridge the gap between our effort and accomplishment (I Jno. 1:7-9).

JOB'S WORDS WITHOUT KNOWLEDGE

Twice Elihu indicted Job for speaking words without knowledge (34:35; 35:16). Is this true? Yes, for God so charged him (38:2) and later he admitted: "I uttered that I understood not; things too wonderful for me, which I knew not" and of this he repented (42:3-6). How had he spoken without knowledge?

He questioned divine justice, though he did not actually charge God foolishly. Elihu accused him of self-righteousness (33:9). Was he guilty? He had rightfully defended himself against his friends' false charges; but evidently he had maintained his innocence to the point of casting a doubt upon divine fairness, for the Almighty asked: "Wilt thou also disannul my judgment? wilt thou condemn me, that thou mayest be righteous?" (40:8).

He concluded that the Lord had become his enemy (10:16, 17; 19:6-12). To the suffering man it seemed that only an enemy would treat him in such a manner. In his distress he cast a reflection upon the Father's mercy and goodness. He thus spoke words without knowledge, and Elihu recognized this as error (33:10-12). Far from being an enemy, the Lord was his Best Friend.

Job stated that his Maker had hid himself and was not to be found: "Behold, I go forward, but he is not there; and backward, but I cannot perceive him. On the left hand, where he doth work, but I cannot behold him: he hideth himself on the right hand, that I cannot see him" (23:8,9). The depressed man honestly thought this to be true; but it was words without knowledge, for God was ever-present (Acts 17:27,28).

Though Job erred in these points, he was more accurate in his understanding of the heavenly Father than were Eliphaz, Bildad and Zophar (42:7).

MULTIPLIED WORDS WITHOUT KNOWLEDGE

Words. Words. Words. They fill the world every day. And the majority spoken over the earth today were words without knowledge. Is this a rash or exaggerated statement? We believe not. Men often "multiplieth words without knowledge" (35:16). Think about the various areas of human endeavor.

In the realm of religion, this day many words were spoken and written. How many of them were words without knowledge? Most of them. Truth is not contradictory, but most of the words used today concerning spiritual matters were contradictory — not only at variance one with another, but also at variance with the word of God. Job's mistake was in the field of religion. He did not intend to do so, but later found that he had spoken without sufficient understanding. This is true of all who charge God foolishly or teach any kind of false doctrine. Some teachers in the first century were guilty of this error (I Tim. 1:7).

In the realm of science, scientists themselves freely admit that many things taught in the past are now known to be false. Thus, they were words without knowledge. Likewise, that which is accepted today may be considered obsolete or false tomorrow. However, truth in science, as well as truth in religion, never changes. It does not fluctuate. That which was truth yesterday is still truth today in either field. False teachings constitute words without knowledge; but in viewing man's history through the ages, evidence testifies that more words have been spoken without knowledge than with knowledge.

You may extend this principle to cover every area of study which mankind pursues.

In the realm of human relationships, or man's dealings with his fellowman, most of the words spoken today were actually words without knowledge. No statement can go through three mouths without alteration. Therefore, most things told every day concerning other people are untrue. They simply didn't happen like they are told. Even if a statement should be half true, beware, for you may have taken the altered half. The three friends spoke many truths to Job, but they also spoke words which never should have been uttered. They simply didn't know what they were talking about part of the time. Remaining silent would have been far better.

Yes, silence can truly be golden — for so often all of us speak when we should be silent. "Let thy speech be better than silence, or be silent" — Dionysius. How careful we must be, lest we should speak words without knowledge.

REVIEW EXERCISE

1. How did Elihu describe the way he felt? ....

....

2. Why did he say he had refrained from speaking sooner? ....

....

3. (T or F) Elderly people are always wise.

4. What would happen if God should decide to "gather unto himself his spirit and his breath"? ....

5. When God chastens his children, what is the purpose? (33:29,30)

....

....

6. "If thou ...., what doest thou against him? or if thy transgressions be multiplied, what doest thou unto him? If thou be ...., what givest thou him? or what receiveth he of ....?"

7. How had Job spoken words without knowledge? ....

....

....

8. What did Job say when he realized his error? ....

....

9. How does I Tim. 1:7 describe some who were teachers? ....

....

FOR THOUGHT OR DISCUSSION

1. If Elihu had been more concerned with retaining man's favor than with upholding truth, would he have rebuked such prominent men as Job and his three friends? See 32:20-22. This took great courage on the young man's part, just as it did for John the Baptist to rebuke Herod (Matt. 14:3,4).

2. Beethoven is not on trial before a high school glee club; Shakespeare is not on trial before a high school drama class. Christ was not on trial before Pilate, but rather Pilate was actually on trial before Christ. God and his judgments are not on trial before mere man, but rather man is on trial before God. Consider this thought in the light of Elihu's words in 33:12-14. Also see 9:12 and Dan. 4:35.

IX

Answer If You Can

HAVE you ever flown in an airplane? If so, do you remember the sensation of awe and wonder the first time you looked down upon the vastness of the earth? Do you remember how you felt the first time you looked at the ocean, or saw the immensity of the Grand Canyon? The wondrous majestic works of nature are awe-inspiring. They bear emphatic and undeniable testimony of man's helplessness when contrasted with the Power that controls the universe.

This same soul-stirring and profound amazement envelops us as we read the glorious climax of the Book of Job. If we could actually see the magnificent drama unfold before our eyes, we would stand with reverence as the Voice of Heaven speaks from the midst of a whirlwind. Job had asked for answers. Instead, he got questions — rhetorical questions leveled at him in rapid-fire succession with such force that he, the suffering and confused man, was brought prostrate before his Interrogator.

"Stand up like a man, Job, and I have some things to ask you. Listen, and answer if you can," said the Almighty. These questions, which we shall paraphrase and group by subjects to promote ease of study, should be carefully studied by every person. They will strengthen the faith of any child of God. They should shake any atheist or skeptic into a realization that his position is false, unreasonable and untenable. For four chapters (38-41) God points out numerous things which are either unknowable or impossible in the realm of human endeavor. The full impact is this: if man is so ignorant and weak concerning all things upon the earth, both mind and matter, how can he presume to question or to tell the Creator how to rule in spiritual government?

CONCERNING THE UNIVERSE — ITS ORIGIN AND OPERATION

"Job, where were you when I laid the foundations of the earth? Who planned the measure of it? Upon what is it fastened? Who laid the cornerstone of it?" (38:4-7). Scientists tell us that if the earth were not just the size it is and placed where it is, life for us would be impossible. If it were any closer to the sun, life would be burned; if it were any farther, life would freeze. Who placed it upon its axis, determined its size and location, and made possible the conditions of life?

"Who shut up the sea with doors, so that it can come only so far?" (38:8-11). Who keeps the water from overrunning the whole earth when the tides come in?

"Have you ever made a morning? Have you caused light to come and displace darkness?" (38:12-15). The most brilliant genius in the world can never make a morning. Have you ever watched the Almighty make one? If so, you have witnessed a testimony of his power as the dull gray slowly gives way to varied tints and hues until they blend into one full-orbed burst of light. As the sun moves majestically into the heavens, it tells of divine Presence and Power.

In the holy hush of the early dawn
I hear a Voice —
"I am with you all the day,
Rejoice! Rejoice!"

"Have you ever entered into the springs of the sea? Have you walked on the depths of the sea?" (38:16). There is

still so much man does not know about the sea and the wonders of marine life.

"Do you know where light dwells? Do you know where darkness dwells? Are you old enough to know this? Or were light and darkness already in existence before you were born?" (38:19-21). What is light? Not just the sun's rays, for light existed before the sun — as revealed in Genesis 1:3 and now admitted by scientists. What is darkness? The mere absence of light, we are told. What is light? Man still does not know, and he has absolutely no control over the light which comes and displaces the darkness of the night.

"Have you unlocked all the treasures of the snow? or of the hail?" (38:22,23). Water is one of the marvels of nature. It is unique, different from any other substance. Its precipitation upon the earth in the form of rain, hail and snow is necessary to our existence. The nature of snow and hail is wonderful and amazing. In many parts of the world, snow blankets the earth and prevents crops from being destroyed by cold winter air. Snowflakes are fascinating. No two are alike, and each is a marvel of symmetry and beauty. Scientists admit that they still have not unlocked all the treasures within snow and hail.

"Who causes the rain in the wilderness and desolate places where no man is?" (38:25-28). Rain comes to these places. By whose power? Not man's.

"From whence comes ice, which hides the waters like a stone when the face of the deep is frozen?" (38:29,30). Water is the only substance which is lighter when frozen. Ice forms a layer of protection over the water and keeps marine life from freezing. Man is at a loss to understand all the peculiar qualities of water. Nobody knows why two gases combine to make a liquid, or why that liquid can be frozen and fall from the skies like a rock, or be used to freeze our food, or why the

same liquid can be heated to power a locomotive. But we still drink it to sustain life and use it for our comfort and welfare. The only explanation is that the unique nature of water was planned by a Superior Wisdom for a reason.

"Do you control the various constellations in the heavens? Do you control the grouping of the stars? Do you know the laws that govern the heavens?" (30:31-33). Edward Young, the noted writer, said: "An undevout astronomer is mad." A study of the universe produces faith, not doubt, to the intellectually honest inquirer. Sir Isaac Newton discovered that gravity is essential to the orderly operation of the whole universe, but he could neither comprehend nor explain what gravity is. Scientists today can do no better. You may drop any object and it goes downward. Why does it not go upward? Because of gravity. What is gravity? It cannot be seen, tasted, smelled, felt or heard — in other words, not measurable by the five senses. Yet it is so real that everyone, even an atheist, knows that if it failed to operate, the world would be destroyed.

Man is limited to finding out the laws that govern the universe. He is absolutely powerless either to make or to change those laws. Man can create nothing. He can only discover and use that which has already been created. Of what then has he to boast? His arrogance would oftentimes be laughable, if it were not so tragic.

"Do you have power over the clouds or the lightning? Can you send lightning where you want it to go?" (38:34,35). "Do you control the bottles of heaven, when drought has caused the dust to grow together in clods upon the earth?" (38:37,38).

CONCERNING DEATH

"Have the gates of death been opened to you? Have you

seen the doors of the shadow of death?" (38:17). Man is helpless in the presence of death. What is death? What is life? No human being knows. Yet everybody must admit that both are very real. You may step on a crawling insect. Something goes from that body, something man can never replace. You may sit beside a dear one and watch as the spirit leaves the body. You cannot see it. No man, no matter how brilliant, can cause the spirit to return to the body. Man can put the ingredients together and make an egg which looks natural, but he cannot make it hatch.

Thus, man is powerless over life or death. Then how can anyone be an atheist? The very facts of life and death which we witness every day testify of a Superior Power.

CONCERNING THE MIND OF MAN

"Who put wisdom in the inward parts? Or who has given understanding to the heart?" (38:36). Even if it were possible for man's body to evolve by mere chance, from whence came his intelligence? His ability to reason, to plan, to think? We know we have this power, but no man can comprehend it. The materialist finds himself in a ridiculous position. What is a thought? What color is it? How much does it weigh? How does one differ from another? Everyone knows that man has an invisible part which is the source, the motivation, of every action.

Many men have spent lifetimes studying the human mind, only to conclude that most things concerning it are still incomprehensible. This is still further testimony of a Superior Intelligence.

CONCERNING ANIMALS, FOWLS, AND SEA LIFE

"Who provides food for the lions and the ravens?" (38: 39-41).

"Do you know when the wild goats and the deer bring forth their young?" (39:1-4).

"Who made the wild ass and gave him his freedom?" (39: 5-8).

"Can you bind the unicorn and make him plough for you?" (39:10-12). Evidently this has reference to the wild ox with his ferocious and untamable nature.

"Did you give the beautiful wings to the peacocks, or the feathers to the ostrich?" (39:13-18). Then follows a fascinating and accurate description of the ostrich. It is most interesting to compare this passage with the characteristics given in any current authoritative work. The World Book Encyclopedia states that the ostrich is the most stupid of all creatures. This is not surprising, for "God deprived her of wisdom." A man can stretch an ostrich head over his hand and freely go among them and capture them. An ostrich will put her head into a bush and think nobody sees her. She lays her eggs and then many times goes away, not bothering to incubate them at all. It may be that some other ostrich will come along and hatch part of them. "She is hardened against her young ones, as though they were not hers." It is not unusual for her to abandon her young. "She scorneth the horse and his rider." An ostrich can outrun a horse as she goes in a half-running, half-flying manner. It has been said that King Cyrus issued a standing offer of one hundred camels for any horse which could outrun an ostrich. One has never been found.

"Have you given the horse his strength and courage?" (39: 19-25). The characteristics of the horse are given in one of the most vivid portrayals.

"Does the hawk fly by your wisdom, and stretch her wings toward the south?" (39:26).

"Does the eagle fly by your command as she makes her home high in the rocks?" (39:27-30).

"Behold now behemoth, which I made" (40:15-24). Some have thought this to mean the hippopotamus or the elephant. However, the detailed description does not accurately fit any animal now in existence and therefore probably has reference to a mammoth animal now extinct. Much has been said of "prehistoric animals." Actually, from one viewpoint, there is no such thing — for God's word gives a history of the first animals. However, some species have become extinct, and this Scripture corresponds with this known fact. From the viewpoint of human history, such would be considered "prehistoric."

"Canst thou draw out leviathan with a hook?" (41:1). The entire chapter is devoted to an elaborate description of a crowning marvel in the natural world, the leviathan. This has been interpreted to mean either the crocodile or some mammoth sea monster now extinct. It was some creature of such strength and ferocity that it confirmed God's might to the readers of the Book of Job centuries ago.

CONCERNING INSIGHT INTO MAN'S HEART

"Wilt thou also disannul my judgment? Wilt thou condemn me, that thou mayest be righteous?" the Lord asked Job (40:8). Two things conclusively prove man's weakness and the folly of his questioning divine judgment: (1) God's superior power to do all things — "Hast thou an arm like God? or canst thou thunder with a voice like him?" (40:9). (2) God's ability to look into man's heart, to detect such sins as pride, and to punish for them (40:11-13). In effect, he says: "Job, whenever you have the power to do these things, then will I confess that you have the ability to save yourself and to decide spiritual judgments" (40:14). This is a force-

ful warning to everyone who thinks he does not need God, that he can save his own soul through morality and good works alone.

THE CONCLUSION

Jehovah guides in all things. He made the monsters of land and sea and placed each in its natural habitat. He also made the smallest microscopic cell. From the behemoth to the amoeba, all creatures are "fearfully and wonderfully made." He controls everything from the atom to the outermost planet. The same Power also guides in spiritual government. Man's knowledge is so limited in the realm of nature — and how much more in the realm of the spirit. Then how could he presume to question divine judgments? To do so would be to declare himself wiser than God.

As this truth penetrated the mind of Job, his whole perspective was changed and for the first time he began to see both himself and the Lord in their true light: "Now mine eye seeth thee. Wherefore I abhor myself, and repent in dust and ashes" (42:5,6). He was humble and penitent. His doubts melted in the sunlight of a fuller faith — and the latter part of his life was better than the beginning.

REVIEW EXERCISE

1. Of what did God charge Job? (38:2) ....

....

2. What did he then tell him to do? ....

....

3. Who is particularly affected by the coming of the daylight? (38:13). ....

4. Ice which forms over the waters is likened to a ....

5. Give some of the characteristics stated concerning the horse. ....

....

....

6. What was Job's response to the first series of questions? (40:4,5)

....

....

....

7. The behemoth is described as having a tail like a ....,

bones as strong as pieces of .... and bars of ....

8. At the conclusion of the Lord's questioning, what did Job say?

....

....

....

FOR THOUGHT OR DISCUSSION

1. For additional study related to this chapter, see Psalm 104.
2. In some of Cicero's most powerful orations, he used the method of beginning with a series of rhetorical questions. Of course, he did not originate the idea, for it is clearly evident in God's words to Job. Why does this carry such force and impact upon the hearers?
3. "There is an Arab proverb — 'As stupid as an ostrich' — which Arabs justify on five grounds: (1) The ostrich, they say, will swallow iron, stones, leaden bullets, and other things, which injure and sometimes prove fatal to it. (2) When hunted, it thrusts its head into a bush, and imagines that the hunter does not see it. (3) It allows itself to be captured by transparent devices. (4) It neglects its eggs. (5) Its head is small, and contains but a small quantity of brains. To these grounds I may add that in the South-African ostrich-farms, the birds allow themselves to be confined within a certain space by a fence of sticks and string raised about a foot from the ground. They seem to think that they cannot step over it" — G. Rawlinson, *Pulpit Commentary*, Vol. XVI, p. 632.

5. Give some of the characteristics [illegible] concerning the horse. [illegible]

....

....

6. What was the response [illegible] first series of questions? (A. 1:5)

....

....

....

7. The [illegible] described [illegible] ring [illegible] as [illegible]

[illegible] as [illegible]

8. At the conclusion of the [illegible] did [illegible]

....

....

....

FOR THOUGHT OR DISCUSSION

1. For additional study related to this chapter, see [illegible]

2. In some of [illegible] questions, he used the method of beginning [illegible] questions. Of course, [illegible] originate the idea, [illegible] early [illegible] to Job. Why [illegible] such force and impact upon the hearers?

3. There is an Arab [illegible] upon [illegible] A [illegible] on the ground; (1) [illegible] will escape [illegible] bullets, and other [illegible] for and sometimes [illegible] (2) When hunted, [illegible] its head into a bush [illegible] that the hunter does not see it; (3) it [illegible] itself [illegible] (4) it neglects its [illegible] a small quantity of [illegible] the [illegible] the birds allow themselves to be [illegible] raised about [illegible] ground. [illegible] think that they [illegible] Commentary, [illegible] p. [illegible]

X

In the Sunlight

"TELL me a happy story." There is no more beautiful and comforting picture than the calm and victorious end of Job's life. We have followed the man through the darkest days of a grief-stricken heart. The storm subsides, and the sunlight of God's love and concern bursts forth in all its splendor. We see the rewards of a triumphant faith, and our hearts rejoice with this man who has endured so much. As we view the whole of his life, we see the various stages through which many of God's children have also gone in times of severe trials: first, silence and a stunned sense of numbness; then a period of questioning, restlessness, hopelessness and temporary rebellion against circumstances, which in time is resolved by faith into a sense of resignation and submission, culminating in a feeling of peace and serenity.

Anchors in the Storm

Job was deprived of all he *had,* but he could not be robbed of all he *was* — that which he had built into his spirit could not be touched. Health, wealth, family and friends were gone, but the anchors with which he had secured his whole life held firm.

"I know." Much he did not know, but by the eye of faith he could see some things for sure: "I know that my redeemer liveth . . . and after my skin, even this body is destroyed, then without my flesh shall I see God" (19:25,26, A.S.V.). His faith produced hope, and hope is the anchor of the soul (Heb. 6:19). William Ellery Channing expressed it like this:

> I laugh, for hope hath happy place with me;
> If my bark sinks, 'tis to another sea.

"He knows." Our knowledge is limited, but God's is not. What Job lacked in understanding was overcome by his assurance that: "He knoweth the way that I take" (23:10). I can't see my way ahead, but *He knows.*

Therefore:

"I will trust him" — "Though he slay me, yet will I trust in him" (13:15).

"I will hold fast my righteousness" — "My righteousness I hold fast, and will not let it go; my heart shall not reproach me so long as I live" (27:6).

"I shall come forth as gold" — "He knoweth the way that I take: when he hath tried me, I shall come forth as gold" (23:10).

These are the anchors which secured his storm-tossed bark, and what Christian needs more? We can know some things for sure; we have assurance that God knows the rest. Then if we will hold fast to his ways, we can say with Job: "I shall come forth as gold."

We must anchor to the eternal and adjust to the temporal. This is our task. Anchors do not stop the storm; they do not still the wind; they do not quieten the waves — but they make it possible for the ship to list with the waves and yet remain secure. When our lives are anchored to the eternal, we can list with the waves of the temporal; and then our little storm-beaten ships can stand anything. On the other hand, if we anchor our lives to people, possessions or profession, the time will come when these will be taken from us, or we will be taken from them. Then we will be left with nothing! Nothing as we step into eternity.

THE TRIUMPH OF FAITH

God takes care of his own. This is a major lesson to be learned from Job. After the storm broke, the whole atmosphere was changed. We can sense an air of new life, of renewed vigor and strength, of freshness and purity. The best and richest part of Job's life came only after the showers of sorrow and despair. The Lord's complete vindication of his servant is seen in the following: (1) Condemnation of his enemies, a renunciation of their false teachings and unjust accusations (42:7,8). (2) Approval of Job's teachings (42:7,8). (3) A recognition of his priestly office (42:9). (4) The bestowal of divine blessings — friends, children and material prosperity (42:10-17).

The rewards of faith are not always seen in this life. Many people have misunderstood God's dealings with man because they have expected every faithful life to end as Job's did — surrounded by earthly joy and comfort. But this is not always true. After many trials and hardships, Paul's life was taken by evil men; yet his victory was no less complete than Job's. This we know: God takes care of his own. Men took Paul's head, but God had his heart, and this is all that mattered! He welcomed an opportunity to go on to his reward (II Tim. 4:6-8). He triumphed over heartache, pain, enemies and a thousand woes to which flesh is heir.

We must triumph while in the midst of trial, not afterwards. It is *within* the furnace of affliction that victory must come. We must triumph over temptation, while in the midst of temptation; over despair while in despair; over suffering while suffering; over sickness in the midst of sickness; over sorrow while sorrowing; and over death while dying.

Last night I heard a robin singing in the rain,
And the raindrop's patter made a sweet refrain,
Making all the sweeter the music of the strain.

So, I thought, when trouble comes, as trouble will,
Why should I stop singing? Just beyond the hill
It may be that sunshine floods the green world still.

He who faces trouble with a heart of cheer
Makes the burden lighter. If there falls a tear,
Sweeter is the cadence in the song we hear.

I have learned your lesson, bird with dappled wing.
Listening to your music with its lilt of spring —
When the storm-cloud darkens, then's *the time* to sing.

— Eben E. Rexford

Victory is possible and necessary. If we would have the joys of heaven, we must be triumphant. "These are they which came out of the great tribulation, and have washed their robes and made them white in the blood of the Lamb" (Rev. 7:14). It is possible. Others have. We can. The saints of yesteryears were human beings with all the weaknesses that characterize us; so their victories are within our reach.

Victory is necessary also for the sake of others. At times when some grief, some disappointment, some burden crushes your heart, you want to sit down and give up. But you cannot afford to. You know that if you fail, others will have to climb over you — or stumble at your failure. This is unthinkable! A mother of two daughters said: "My daily challenge is to so live that my little girls will be perfectly safe walking in my steps." Her daughters' heritage was a beaten path.

TRIUMPH OVER THE DARKNESS OF IGNORANCE

Much sunlight is crowded out of the earth because of the darkness of ignorance. The only means of dispelling this darkness is God's word. "The entrance of thy words giveth light; it giveth understanding to the simple" (Psa. 119:30).

It was God's word which gave Job the light to see his Maker and Preserver in his true likeness. Then he could say: "Now mine eye seeth thee" (42:5), a benevolent Friend, not a cruel tyrant.

TRIUMPH OVER THE DARKNESS OF SIN

Many are struggling in the darkness of despair because of sin. But Christ came that we might have light, light which comes from forgiveness, direction and hope. He is the "Sun of righteousness...with healing in his wings" (Mal. 4:2). Only through him can one be turned "from darkness to light and from the power of Satan unto God" (Acts 26:18).

TRIUMPH OVER THE DARKNESS OF DESPAIR

Try to remember the darkest, stormiest day you have ever seen. The black clouds hovered so close to the earth that your vision was almost completely obscured. There was thunder. There were sheets of rain. Maybe you were scared. When that happened, where was the sun? The same place it has always been. When that happened, where was the blue of the sky? The same place it has always been — just as big and beautiful and refreshing — but you did not see it, because it was above the clouds which shut out your view. But your limited vision had not diminished the power of the sun or narrowed the expanse of the blue.

Despair — whether caused by bereavement, loneliness, disappointment, failure or physical suffering — at times hovers like a black cloud over us and temporarily shuts out the view of everything but the present distress. When that time comes, we must work to overcome the darkness even while walking in the midst of it. How can this be done?

Remember that the blue of the sky is always larger than the cloud, and the sun is still shining. With the eye of faith we can see the sun of God's love and care and help. The bright rays can pierce through the black cloud until finally the terrible darkness is dispelled.

Remember that despair always exaggerates every problem. It makes us prone to overstate the ills of life and to forget the countless hours that we were grateful just to be alive.

When the children of Israel were breaking away from slavery and going toward freedom, they sent spies to survey the land to be conquered. Most of the spies despaired, came back and reported that victory was impossible because of giants in the land. Perhaps the people were large; but to the despondent spies they seemed much larger than they were, and appeared to be unconquerable giants. Two of the spies, however, reached an altogether different conclusion. They said: "We can win. We will conquer." Why? They believed that the power within them, coupled with the Power above them, was sufficient to conquer any problem before them. However, the people followed the debilitating advice of the ten spies; and as a result of their unbelief, the Lord barred them from the promised land (Num. 13 and 14).

Remember that life goes in cycles, a series of ups and downs. It does not run in a smooth, even line — for anybody. Even the sun has a sinking spell every night, but it rises again the next morning. Thus. one who expects to live continually on top of sun-embroidered clouds will necessarily be disappointed. Understanding this, when the "down" days come, we should recall what our calm and healthy judgment told us on "up" days. Remember: the dark and morbid feelings are transitory; refuse to judge all of life by them.

Keep your eyes on the eternal. The only way to keep from being frustrated by short-range failures and problems is to have long-range goals. When we view this life against the backdrop of eternity, our whole perspective is changed. It is so comforting to know that though the outward being weakens, the inward being can become stronger, more radiant day by day (II Cor. 4:16-18).

Remember that your Helper is Omnipotent. No person alone can conquer despair. Only divine aid keeps us from sinking beneath life's ills. There are griefs which cannot be healed by man — diseases which no medicine can heal, sorrows which no human aid can touch, despair of guilt which no man can erase, the realization of a wasted life which no man can reclaim. At such times human words, no matter how cheering and comforting, only temporarily draw a sufferer's mind from his sorrow; but the wound has not healed, and from it sorrow returns like a swelling tide. Every person reaches depths to which nobody, absolutely nobody, can go with him. One who tries to live without God then has no helper to lift him from his hopelessness.

The righteous, however, have the comforting assurance: "God is our refuge and strength, a very present help in trouble. Therefore will not we fear, though the earth be removed, and though the mountains be carried into the midst of the sea" (Psa. 46:1,2). "Casting all your care upon him" (I Pet. 5:7). This includes prayer, calling upon our Omnipotent Helper. With his aid we can conquer despair, even though our strength is small. We are "kept by the power of God through faith unto salvation" (I Pet. 1:5).

Faith, then, is our part of the conquest — with an obedient faith we find personal comfort and hope in our Father's precious promises, enough to say: "This promise is mine." This is the faith which sustained the Psalmist: "I had fainted, unless I had believed" (Psa. 27:13).

Gratitude is one of the most powerful gloom-chasers. For the chronic complainer, one who always looks at what he lacks instead of what he has, the future holds nothing but darkness. How often do we count our blessings? A lovely elderly Christian said: "I spend the first ten minutes every morning thanking God that I am alive." And one man said,

"I have learned that if I can just live through today, I have a chance to work out my problems." We need gratitude not only for bright days but also for dark days, realizing that they too have their opportunities and blessings.

The brook would lose its song
If you removed the rocks.

A little blind boy who was returning from the circus commented: "I felt so sorry for those deaf children who were there. They couldn't hear the band play, and they couldn't hear the thud, thud of the elephant as he went by." Though he lacked the precious gift of sight, he possessed in full measure the grateful heart! He could have looked upon his limitations with self-pity. Rather, he looked upon his blessings with gratitude. Robert Louis Stevenson said: "The man who forgets to be thankful has fallen asleep in life."

TRIUMPH OVER THE DARKNESS OF DEATH

"Yea, though I walk through the valley of the shadow of death, I will fear no evil." Why? Because "the Lord is my shepherd." Not was. Not will be. But is.

We stood by the bed of a Christian friend in terminal stages of a fatal disease. She took our hands and looked up at us with brown eyes which showed no tears. Thoughtfully and deliberately she talked: "You know, I've been through some awfully hard places in my life, and the Lord has always seen me through and delivered me from problems which seemed too heavy to bear. And he will see me through this one — only this time he will deliver me by way of death." Never have I witnessed more implicit faith and quiet courage. From her heroic spirit all of us gained much strength and encouragement during her long months in the hospital. She continued: "I do not feel sorry for myself, and I do not ask why this has happened to me. It has happened to many others. Why should

I be exempt? All I ask is that I may have the strength to die with dignity as a Christian should. The Lord will take care of the rest." She talked freely of heaven and her plans to go there very soon. Though the waves had oftentimes lashed hard against her little bark, she had anchored it firmly in the eternal and now she was ready to cross the divide which separates time from eternity. Hers was a triumphant faith.

So it was with Job.

So it will be with every faithful child of God.

REVIEW EXERCISE

1. List some of the anchors which held Job in the midst of his storm.

....

....

....

2. How does Revelation 7:14 describe those who will enter heaven?

....

....

How does one wash his robes in the blood of the Lamb? (Rom. 6:3, 4) ....

3. What did God do for Job at the end of his trial? ....

....

4. What did Job's family and friends do? ....

....

5. Job came to a full knowledge of God through ....

6. Who is the "Sun of righteousness"? ....

7. According to Psalm 46:1,2, why should we not fear? ....

....

FOR THOUGHT OR DISCUSSION

1. The following words of writer James Smetham are worthy of careful consideration:

   > I think I can trace every scrap of sorrow in my life to simple unbelief. How could I be anything but happy if I believed always that all the past is forgiven, and all the present furnished with power, and all the future bright with hope because of the same abiding facts which do not change with my mood, do not stumble because I totter and stagger at the promise through unbelief, but stand firm and clear with their peaks of pearl cleaving the air of eternity, and the bases of their hills rooted unfathomably in the Rock of God. Mont Blanc does not become a phantom or a mist because a climber grows dizzy on its side.

2. There are weights which are not sins within themselves, but which can actually lead to sin. Is not despondency one of these? It can impair our usefulness and cause us to sin by neglecting duties and misusing time.

3. If the dark cloud of despair has ever hovered over you, then remember that the same may be true of any person you meet every day. Such a one may be tottering on the very brink of total despair which the world knows nothing of. If a friend seems cool or not as friendly as usual, this may be the reason. This thought should prompt all of us to be more tolerant and understanding of each other.

XI

Why?

AN atheist once said to a believer: "If there is a God, how do you account for all the suffering in the world?" The believer replied: "If there is no God, how do *you* account for it?" Death, pain, sorrow, suffering of the innocent, poverty, disappointments — these cover the earth. Every thinking person has asked: "Why?" Job asked, "Why?" He complained not so much about what happened to him as he did his inability to understand the reason. It was not the questioning of an atheist but the cries wrung from the heart of God's child.

The problem of human suffering is so complex that perhaps several things are involved in each case, rather than one single explanation. We certainly would not presume to know all the causes in any given problem, lest we should be guilty of Job's mistake: "Therefore have I uttered that I understood not; things too wonderful for me, which I knew not" (42:3). The Book of Job sheds some light on the mystery of adversity. Christ gave additional light. Yet, after carefully studying every truth available, there is still so much we cannot know.

SIN, SUFFERING AND SATAN

In a basic and universal sense, sin is the cause of all suffering. God made all things good (Gen. 1:31). Satan brought sin and suffering into the world. Therefore, if agonizing heartache should tempt us to cry out in bitterness and antagonism against someone, it should be directed against Satan, not God.

However, as forcefully taught by the life of Job, this does

not mean that a specific case of suffering is the result of a specific or personal sin. Many other aspects of adversity must be considered.

WHAT IS GOD'S WILL?

Perhaps one of the most misused and misunderstood phrases is this: "It's God's will." Some have used it in an attempt to explain all joys and sorrows on earth. But it needs much study and clarification. It has actually turned some completely from God. For example, a child wanders into the street and is killed by a passing automobile. In attempting to console grief-stricken parents, someone may say, "It's God's will." Such a statement may strain the sorrowing parents' faith to the breaking point, for they will naturally question: "Why would God will that our precious one be snatched from us so cruelly?" Was it God's will? The term "God's will" must be clarified. There is a difference between the Father's intentional will and his permissive will.

God's intentional will. The Creator made man and for his good and happiness set in order all laws, both physical and spiritual, desiring that his offspring should obey them and be blessed thereby.

God's permissive will. He controls all things in heaven and earth. Nothing is done — either by man or Satan — without his permission. However, he made man with the power of choice, a freedom of will. Without this, the creature would not be in the image of the Creator, but rather as an animal or a machine. Therefore, man can choose to violate divine laws; and when he does, the Father permits the consequences.

Was it God's will for Job to suffer? Yes and no. It was not his intentional will — for he did not plan it; but under the circumstances, he permitted it.

In studying this more fully, adversity may be thus classified: (1) trouble man brings upon himself, (2) trouble brought on by others, and (3) tribulation which is the chastening of the Father.

TROUBLE MAN BRINGS UPON HIMSELF

Anytime divine laws are violated — whether physical or spiritual — the consequences will come. This violation may be either (1) through deliberate will, or (2) through carelessness, or (3) through ignorance. Thus, much suffering of both body and spirit is that which man brings upon himself. Understanding this can increase our foresight and avoid many heartaches.

Physical laws were ordained for our good. For instance, the law of gravitation keeps all things in place on the earth. Suppose, however, that one should go to the top of a tall building and jump. He would die. Because it was God's will? Not his intentional will. Not that God desired it or planned it, but he willed: (1) that man should have freedom of choice and (2) that the law of gravitation should continue to operate. Thus, it was his permissive will. Suppose that he should have temporarily suspended the law of gravitation just to save one life. Can you visualize how many other lives would have been destroyed as a result? Through the law of gravitation God permitted Judas to hang himself (Matt. 27:3-5).

Through carelessness, divine physical laws may be violated. Suppose one gets into a car, speeds down the street and carelessly hits another car. It may bring death to himself and to others. Is this God's will? Not his intentional will. He does not intend for man to carelessly kill. It is his permissive will because he has instituted the law of force for man's good. This decrees that when a stronger object is pitted against a weaker object, the weaker object must give way to the force. We can depend upon this law. Without it, man could never hammer a nail into a board to build himself a house. Suppose that our Father should temporarily suspend the law of force just to protect some careless driver. Can you visualize the chaos it would create in all the universe? Fire is another blessing, but man can carelessly misuse it and bring great destruction, heartache and suffering. Not because God wills it, but because he permits freedom of choice.

Through ignorance or a failure to use physical laws, man causes much suffering. Our Creator instituted physical and economic laws whereby life-sustaining food can be grown. Yet in some parts of the world people are starving, including innocent children, because of a failure to apply these laws — either through ignorance or laziness.

Divine laws of health regulate man's well-being. If these laws are violated — either deliberately, carelessly or ignorantly — the consequences will come. Because of natural law God allowed Epaphroditus to become ill (Phil. 2:25-28). Of course, we know: "It is appointed unto man once to die" (Heb. 9:27). These bodies were never meant for an eternal existence, and in time they will weaken and perish. We understand this. But when life is shortened by disease or accident, then we are prone to ask why.

Pain is a preserver of life, a part of natural law for man's good. It is a warning signal. Thus, when natural law is broken, pain often arrests us and turns us back in the right direction. For instance, a child may place his hand in a fire. If there were no pain, he could be destroyed and never realize it. The pain serves as a protector and preserver by causing him instinctively to draw back. Pain helps to determine the location and intensity of disease or injury, and all physicians recognize that it was ordained by a beneficent Creator not to harm but to preserve life. If he should have suspended this law temporarily just for the comfort of his child Job, think how many others could have been destroyed in the process.

Man often violates natural law by the use of foreign and destructive elements such as alcohol and harmful drugs (Prov. 23:29-32). Then when the body is writhing in the pain of some resulting degenerative disease, one may cry out: "Why has God done this to me?" Of course, God did not do it. He permits man to destroy himself if he wants to.

Spiritual laws are just as fixed and binding. As in the physical realm, man reaps what he sows. Eliphaz stated: "Even as I have seen, they that plow iniquity, and sow wickedness, reap the same" (4:8). This is true. The New Testament teaches: "Be not deceived; God is not mocked: for whatsoever a man soweth, that shall he also reap. For he that soweth to his flesh shall of the flesh reap corruption; but he that soweth to the Spirit shall of the Spirit reap life everlasting" (Gal. 6:7,8).

The chief argument of Eliphaz, Bildad and Zophar was that sin brings suffering. Yet the Almighty rebuked them and required them to repent of their teachings. Why? They misapplied this principle. They were reasoning: "Job, your adversity is proof that you have sown sin." They were using it to teach that one who sows spiritual iniquity will reap physical calamity. This is a false teaching. It was a belief still prevalent in Christ's day, and he refuted it (Jno. 9:2,3).

Man who sows sin will reap corruption, spiritual corruption. Part of the reaping is in this life. Most of it will be in the next world. Even in this life, however, man brings much sorrow upon himself by a violation of spiritual laws.

For instance, the misuse of the tongue may cause one to be embroiled in constant turmoil and strife — sorrow brought on oneself by breaking a divine spiritual law. One who allows the heart to become filled with envy, hatred or unforgiveness will spend many wretched days — anguish of spirit brought upon himself. This principle is true of many other sins.

TROUBLE BROUGHT ON BY OTHERS

Much adversity, both of body and spirit, comes not from one's own conduct but from the actions of others. In the physical realm this accounts for much suffering of the young and innocent. Children may perish with starvation because of indolent parents, or endure physical injury at the hands of brutal parents. Every day's paper exclaims in bold headlines that the innocent suffer because of the guilty. A criminal takes a man's life, leaving his wife and children with years of loneliness and burdens to bear — heartaches all brought on by someone else's sin. Truly, "Man's inhumanity to man makes countless thousands mourn." This is a major cause of sorrow that fills the earth. In wars the innocent suffer because of the guilty. Some have asked: "Why does not God stop such evil?" If he did, he would deny all mankind the freedom of choice, and we would not want that. Wars come from man's choice, the wrong one (Jas. 4:1).

Christ's hardships were not of his own making. He lived in the midst of turmoil, disappointments, sorrow, persecution and finally the most intense physical suffering. Why? Not because of sin he had committed, but because of the sins of others. Righteousness did not exempt him from heartaches — he wept (Jno. 11:35), or from physical pain — he thirsted (Jno. 19:28). He suffered the innocent for the guilty, which is, more or less, the fate of humanity.

Many suffer because they are righteous. "The wicked plotteth against the just, and gnasheth upon him with his teeth" (Psa. 37:12). Envy develops a decay within the heart which grows until it reaches murderous proportions. Envy took the life of

Abel. If he had not been righteous, Cain would have had no desire to kill him (Gen. 4:1-8). If Joseph had not been better than his brethren, they would have felt no need to do away with him. If Job had not been godly, Satan would have felt no urge to challenge him to a duel and attempt to destroy him.

Yes, so much anguish comes from others' sins. In time this will be experienced by every righteous person. The difficult thing is: (1) to refrain from retaliation, and (2) to refrain from bitterness. If Satan can lead us into either of these sins, he has achieved a marked victory.

THE CHASTENING OF THE LORD

This is another aspect of our trials. "For whom the Lord loveth he chasteneth" (Heb. 12:6).

"Why?" "For our profit" — because he loves us, as discussed later.

"How?" No one knows for sure. Abraham was tested directly (Gen. 22:1-14). Job was tested when Satan was permitted to do so, but God also had a part in it (2:3). From Satan's viewpoint, it was a tempting. From the Father's viewpoint, it was a testing. What is the difference? The word tempt means to try to lure one into sin. God does not do this (Jas. 1:13). He was not wanting Job to sin; he was wanting him to withstand the temptation. The Lord allowed Satan to try the faith of Paul (II Cor. 12:7).

Thus, when tribulations come our way, how can we know whether we are being tempted by Satan or chastened by God? We cannot. There is no possible way to know. Job never knew.

"What?" This is the most important question. When some hardship comes upon us, oftentimes we are prone to lie down

and groan in the *why* of it. It is far more important for us to get up and look at the *what.* We can never fully know why many things happen. If so, it would no longer be a walk of faith. This being true, when heartaches descend like an avalanche, let's cry not so much, "*Why,* Lord?" as we do "*What,* Lord?" (1) "*What,* Lord, if anything, can I do to remedy the trouble?" (2) "*What,* Lord, would you have me to learn from this experience?" Whether trouble originates with Satan's temptation or God's chastening, it can still be used for our profit.

In analyzing our troubles and trying to decide what course to follow now and in the future, it is helpful to classify them:

(1) Some can be avoided.

(2) Others can be cured.

(3) The rest can be endured.

(4) All can be used for our profit.

REVIEW EXERCISE

1. What are the causes of tribulation, as given in this lesson?

(1) ....

(2) ....

(3) ....

2. "They that plow ...., and sow ...., reap the same."

3. One who sows to the flesh will reap ....

Does this refer to physical or spiritual reaping?

4. What did Christ say concerning the man who was born blind?

....

....

5. What was wrong with the philosophy of the three friends? ....

....

....

6. What was the cause of Christ's hardships? ....

7. Why did Cain dislike Abel? ....

8. "The wicked .... the just."

9. (T or F) God tempts men to do evil.

10. Whom does the Lord chasten? ....

11. It has been suggested that it would be helpful to classify our troubles: (1) ....

(2) ....

(3) ....

(4) ....

FOR THOUGHT OR DISCUSSION

1. Though tribulation may be caused by Satan's agents, can God help to turn it into a victory? Joseph did. His brethren deliberately sinned against him, and therefore we know that God did not prompt their actions. However, Joseph used their evil to accomplish good, for many years later he said to his brethren: "Ye thought evil against me: but God meant it for good, to bring to pass, as it is this day, to save much people alive" (Gen. 50:20).

2. Wars are caused by man's sins, not by God. However, has the Lord helped Christians to use this evil to promote good by spreading the gospel to many parts of the world?

XII

The Dark Mile

IN Scotland there is a narrow and dangerous mountain road. There is no way around it, and thus many must travel it to reach their homes. So many have lost their lives in the treacherous passageway that the people call it "the dark mile."

So it is with us. Between here and our eternal home, we must travel the dark mile — perhaps many times. There will be no way around it. We will have to go through it to reach home. It is in this treacherous darkness that many souls become spiritual casualties on their journey to heaven. It will fortify and strengthen us to travel the dark mile safely, if we will learn all we can about the nature of adversity. God's word teaches that tribulations are (1) certain, (2) uncertain, (3) painful, (4) temporary and (5) beneficial.

Adversity Is Certain

Experience teaches that no person is exempt from hardships. Trouble comes to the righteous and wicked, the young and old, the rich and poor. We see it all around us.

God's revelation tells us to expect trouble. Thus, no child of God should ever be surprised when trials come. We should be expecting them, confident that they will come. The Book of Job teaches this: "Yet man is born unto trouble, as the sparks fly upward" (5:7). "Man that is born of woman is of few days and full of trouble" (14:1).

Some have thought that the power of God in a human life should lift one above all trials. Actually it brings one directly into conflicts and struggles. Confirmation of this truth is demonstrated in the life of Paul, the great man of God. On his missionary journey to Rome, one might expect divine aid to lift him above the tempests and the enemies. On the contrary, it was one long hard fight — with persecuting Jews, venomous vipers, storms at sea and a narrow escape from a watery grave.

Moses fully understood this principle, but he chose "rather to suffer affliction with the people of God, than to enjoy the pleasures of sin for a season" (Heb. 11:25).

Christians are taught to expect hardships. "When ye do well, and suffer for it, ye take it patiently, this is acceptable with God" (I Pet. 2:20). "But and if ye suffer for righteousness sake, happy are ye... for it is better, if the will of God be so, that ye suffer for well doing, than for evil doing" (I Pet. 3:14,17). "For unto you it is given in the behalf of Christ, not only to believe on him, but also to suffer for his sake" (Phil. 1:29). "Verily, verily, I say unto you, that ye shall weep and lament, but the world shall rejoice" (Jno. 16: 20-22). "Yea, all that will live godly in Christ Jesus shall suffer persecution" (II Tim. 3:12).

It is not possible for a sober-minded Christian to avoid heartaches; for he will not only bear his own problems, but must also be grieved by the evil and suffering all about him. The deeper one's insight, the deeper his sorrow for the world's problems. This is the reason Christ wept over lost souls. "For in wisdom is much grief: and he that increaseth knowledge increaseth sorrow" (Eccl. 1:18). Paul was so grieved over the lost state of his kinsmen that he said, "I have great heaviness and continual sorrow in my heart" (Rom. 9:2).

TRIBULATIONS ARE UNCERTAIN

Trials are sure to come, yet they are most uncertain.

Uncertain as to time. "Whereas ye know not what shall be on the morrow. For what is your life? It is even a vapor, that appeareth for a little time, and then vanisheth away. For that ye ought to say, If the Lord will, we shall live, and do this or that" (Jas. 4:14,15). Yes, life can change in a hurry. It did for Job. Tomorrow's sun may find us enveloped in a heartache which we cannot now imagine. Our Father's goodness veils the future from us; for if tomorrow's problems should be added to today's, we would be unable to bear them.

Uncertain as to kind. We know not what form of trial we may be called upon to bear.

Uncertain as to length. To a sufferer, time can be the most comforting friend or the cruelest foe. It is a gift from God which heals many hurts and eases others. On the other hand, time is one of the hardest aspects of suffering. When one can foresee no end to a problem, it is then that hopelessness and despair set in. For example, you can stand the dentist's drill for awhile — but how would you feel if you faced the prospect of enduring it day and night the rest of your life?

Patience is defined as "endurance or perseverance." Sometimes we think of patience as a passive thing. We envision one waiting, doing nothing. However, we are commanded to "run with patience the race that is set before us" (Heb. 12:1) — and this is even harder. This requires activity. This means working at the tasks before us, even while enduring great sorrows. We cannot sit and wait for deliverance *from* the furnace of affliction. We must work while *in* the furnace.

Paul did, or else he would have accomplished nothing. His thorn in the flesh was constant. He had to learn to live with it, for God did not promise ever to remove it. When deliverance did not come, he still served the Lord with diligence and thankfulness. This is running with patience.

You have seen women devote a lifetime to the care of an

invalid child. You have seen others bury a most beloved companion and then turn their hands to the exacting challenge of faithfully rearing fatherless children, all the time carrying in their hearts a sorrow never lifted. You have seen men go about daily tasks, assuming heavy responsibilities, with never a word of complaint about crosses almost too heavy to bear. Some problems have no solution in this life. Yet many heroically bear them, all the time serving the Lord — truly, this is running with patience.

TRIALS ARE PAINFUL

We are human. Though we may understand that trials can be a sign of God's love, beneficial and necessary to our spiritual growth, they are still painful. Paul endured the severest bonds and afflictions, and he said: "None of these things move me." You will notice he did not say: "None of these things hurt me." Of course they hurt. His heart bled. But the hurt did not move him away from the Father.

Our Creator understands pain — both of body and spirit — for he speaks of his children who are "in heaviness through manifold temptations" (I Pet. 1:6); and further says, "Now no chastening for the present seemeth to be joyous, but grievous" (Heb. 12:11). He did not rebuke Job for his despondency and anguished cries. He knew that his servant was going through the refiner's fire, and being in the midst of fire cannot be at the time pleasant. As Christ neared the cross, he "began to be sorrowful and very heavy. Then saith he unto them, My soul is exceeding sorrowful, even unto death" (Matt. 26: 37,38). Yes, our heavenly Father understands the pain of a heavy heart. He was with Job. He was with Christ. He is with us, whatever our suffering.

TRIBULATIONS ARE TEMPORARY

We have only one earthly life and it is very dear to us. For this reason, it is natural to put too much emphasis upon it. *The Christian, however, learns to view this life against the backdrop of eternity.* Then our time here becomes only a very small part of the whole. The humanists and materialists charge that this is a morbid view, that it makes this life only a tragic prelude to be stoically and grimly endured. Quite to the contrary, this adds real sweetness and meaning to all human relationships, and causes the Christian to be far more concerned with human suffering than the humanist can ever be. If there is no after-life, what balm has the humanist to offer a burdened or suffering soul? None whatsoever.

The Christian understands that hardships are fleeting and insignificant when compared with eternity. This offers strength and comfort never possible from a this-world-only philosophy. "If so be that we suffer with him, that we may also be glorified together. For I reckon that the sufferings of this present time are not worthy to be compared with the glory which shall be revealed in us" (Rom. 8:17,18).

> **When the crown is won at last**
> **Who will count the heartaches past?**

"Wherein ye greatly rejoice, though now for a season, if need be, ye are in heaviness through manifold temptations" (I Pet. 1:6). Whatever the burden, it is but "for a season."

TRIALS ARE BENEFICIAL — "FOR OUR PROFIT"

Since hardships and heartaches are inevitable, it's only smart for us to learn to receive them with the right attitude. By this we benefit ourselves. If we can learn this before the trial comes, it will help to carry us through. When the surgeon's knife is in a patient, it is easy to think the surgeon cruel, rough and unsympathetic; but the patient is not then in a proper state to judge correctly. If, however, he is convinced of the value of surgery beforehand, he can endure tremendous trials.

Railing upon the surgeon in indignation, bitterness or contempt would indeed be a mark of folly, ignorance and ingratitude.

The wrong attitude toward adversity is the thing which destroys, not adversity itself. What is the wrong attitude? (1) To receive it with contempt and indignation, railing at God. (2) To emerge from it in impenitence or bitterness.

What is the right attitude?

An understanding that trials promote our spiritual growth and are thus "for our profit."

> **My son, despise not thou the chastening of the Lord, nor faint when thou art rebuked of him: for whom the Lord loveth he chasteneth, and scourgeth every son whom he receiveth . . . for our profit, that we might be partakers of his holiness (Heb. 12:5-10).**

We understand the value and necessity of discipline in the proper training of a child. How much more essential it is in spiritual development. Godliness is not a gift but an achievement, and one thorn of experience is worth more than a whole briar-patch of warning. Even Christ learned through suffering (Heb. 7:8).

We are still in the process of being made, as the sculptor works with his marble. He must cut here and chisel there, or the stone remains rough, ugly and unpolished. Your present distress may be but a tool in the Father's hand to chisel you for eternity; so do not despise it but rather use its valuable help. An understanding of this principle undergirds our faith in this promise: "And we know that all things work together for good to them that love God, to them who are the called according to his purpose" (Rom. 8:28).

Whatever our hardship, let's remember that it is not to satisfy some whim of our Creator, for he is neither helped by our righteousness nor hurt by our sin, as pointed out by Elihu (35:6,7). We're not doing him a big favor by remaining faithful through trials; he is doing us a favor by teaching us through trials how to be faithful. Why? No sin can enter heaven; only through holiness can we enter — and holiness, spiritual maturity, is not achieved in ease and comfort. This is evident both from observation and divine revelation. There can be no physical growth without exercise. No muscle develops in rest, ease and comfort. Exercise is resistance to pressure. Spiritual exercise is resistance to the pressure of evil and adversity.

When a mother eagle decides that her young should learn to fly, she literally kicks one out of the nest high in the craigs of the rocks. The eaglet starts downward, frightened and struggling, flapping his little untrained wings while falling, falling. The mother eagle soars above him and observes his efforts for awhile. Then she flies underneath the weary eaglet and takes him upon her own wing and bears him again upward.

Our heavenly Father uses this figure of speech in a beautiful and comforting description of his watchful care over his own. "As the eagle stirreth up her nest, fluttereth over her young, spreadeth abroad her wings, taketh them, beareth them on her wings: so the Lord alone did lead him" (Deut. 32:11,12). To strengthen us and fit us for a glorious eternity, he allows us to struggle and try. All the while he is tenderly watching. When the burden seems greater than we can bear, when it seems that we must cease our struggle and fall completely, then our Protector is there to bear us again upward. By this we grow.

Soldiers are not made by fancy uniforms and colorful parades, but rather by marching long with heavy burdens, by fording streams, climbing mountains, and pitting themselves against many obstacles both mental and physical. And each battle increases strength and ability for the next one. So it is with God's soldiers.

> Nearer my God to Thee, nearer to Thee,
> E'en tho' it be a cross that raiseth me.

We sing it. Do we really mean it? Not usually. We would like to be closer to the Father, but oftentimes we rebel at the cross which can lead us there (Matt. 16:24; 10:38).

We are told to rejoice in persecutions (Matt. 5:11,12). Rejoice in persecutions? Is this possible? Paul did. He had learned to "take pleasure in infirmities, in reproaches, in necessities, in persecutions, in distresses for Christ's sake: for when I am weak, then am I strong" (II Cor. 12:7-10). How could he do this? Because he realized that such contributed to his spiritual growth.

Thus, we should pray not for experiences which make us comfortable, but for those which make us strong.

> Is it raining, little flower?
> Be glad of rain;
> Too much sun would wither thee;
> 'Twill shine again.
> The clouds are very black, 'tis true;
> But just behind them shines the blue.
>
> Art thou weary, tender heart?
> Be glad of pain;
> In sorrow sweetest virtues grow,
> As flowers in rain.
> God watches, and thou wilt have sun,
> When clouds their perfect work have done.
>
> — Lucy Larcom

REVIEW EXERCISE

1. (T or F) Moses thought that serving God would be an easy life.

2. What figure of speech did James use to describe the brevity of life? ....

3. "When ye .... and .... for it, ye take it patiently, this is acceptable with God."

4. (T or F) Speaking of his tribulations, Paul said: "None of these things hurt me."

5. Who said, "My soul is exceeding sorrowful"? ....

6. "It is better . . . to suffer for .... than for ...." Scripture: ....

7. How did Job describe man's days upon the earth? ....

8. Why does God chasten his children? ....

9. "If any man will come after me, let him ...., and take up his ...., and follow me."
Scripture: .... What does Christ say concerning those who are unwilling to do this? .... Scripture: ....

10. Paul had so matured spiritually that he had learned to "take pleasure in ...., in ...., in ...., in ...., in .... for Christ's sake: for when I am weak then am I ...." Scripture: ....

FOR THOUGHT OR DISCUSSION

1. God intends for age and adversity to mellow us and cause us to be more useful and more understanding. Mothers and grandmothers will appreciate this about two little boys who were talking. "Wouldn't you hate to wear glasses all the time?" one asked. "No," replied his friend thoughtfully, "not if I had the kind

Grandma wears. You see, she sees how to fix a lot of things, and sees a lot of nice things to do on rainy days. She sees when folks are sad or tired and what'l make 'em feel better. And she always sees what you meant to do, even if you haven't got things just right. I asked her one day how she could see that way all time, and she said it was the way she learned to look at things as she grew older. So I guess it must be her glasses."

2. In our Bible class we studied about the eaglet and the meaning of the Scripture which uses this figure of speech. Several weeks later, one of the ladies said: "I've decided what's happened to me today. I have just been kicked out of that nest again!"

XIII

More Precious Than Gold

WOULD you like to possess a treasure more precious than gold? What is it? A faith which has been tested and proved. Pure gold is obtained only after the refiner's fire has removed all impurities. Far more precious is a pure and strong faith which is possible only after it has been severely tried. All of us would like to have the treasure, but we shrink back from the necessary testing. Job concluded: "When he hath tried me, I shall come forth as gold" (23:10).

To fellow-Christians Peter wrote: "Wherein ye greatly rejoice though now for a season, if need be, ye are in heaviness through manifold temptations: that the trial of your faith, being much more precious than of gold that perisheth, though it be tried with fire, might be found unto praise and honour and glory at the appearing of Jesus Christ" (I Pet. 1:6,7).

Using this same figure of speech, Malachi pictures God as an assayer sitting by his crucible watching: "And he shall sit as a refiner and purifier of silver: and he shall purify the sons of Levi, and purge them as gold and silver, that they may offer unto the Lord an offering in righteousness" (Mal. 3:3).

Fire is used both to purify and to test gold. Even that which is pure may be tested. By the refiner's fire Job was not so much purified as proved. Difficulties show what men are. "If thou faint in the day of adversity, thy strength is small" (Prov. 24:10). By adversity God's children today can be both purified and proved.

The Uses of Adversity

Some non-Christian religions teach how to bear adversity,

but *only Christ teaches how to use it as a cherished blessing to purify, ennoble and lead a step closer to God.* In the familiar words of Shakespeare:

> Sweet are the uses of adversity
> Which like the toad, ugly and venomous
> Wears yet a precious jewel in his head.

Not that adversity is sweet. It never is. But the uses of adversity can be sweet and priceless. The finest china goes through the fire three times; the beauty is brought out and fastened there to stay, a beauty not possible without the firing process.

We never really get over our great sorrows, and our Father does not intend for us to. He intends for their cleansing and refining power to be so completely absorbed into the very fiber of our being that we will never be the same again.

To Achieve Life's Major Purpose

Life's major purpose is not happiness, but holiness. Then happiness is a by-product. One who aims at heaven enjoys the best of earth. One who aims at earth loses both. We may sum up the use of adversity by saying: it helps to achieve the various aspects of spiritual growth which constitute holiness, namely:

Adversity Increases Our Reliance Upon God

When all goes too well, we are lulled into a false sense of security and tend to think we don't need Anybody Else. We can never learn to trust the Lord completely in the midst of comfortable surroundings. But when we are knocked to our knees with a blow so staggering that every nerve winces and our soul cries out in agony, then we look upward. Abraham Lincoln said: "I have been driven many times to my knees by the overwhelming conviction that I had nowhere else to go.

My own wisdom and that of all about me seemed insufficient for that day."

When Peter began to sink in the tumultuous sea, he cried: "Lord, save me" (Matt. 14:30). If his walk had been smooth and successful, he never could have felt so acutely his absolute dependence upon divine aid.

Paul and his co-workers were beset with such trials that they hit the depths of despondency and hopelessness. God permitted it, to teach them reliance upon him (II Cor. 1:8-10).

> Vain is all human help for me;
> I dare not trust an earthly prop!
> My sole reliance is in thee;
> Thou art my Hope.
> — Elliott

TRIALS TEACH SUBMISSION TO DIVINE WILL

Of Christ it is said: "Though he were a Son, yet learned he obedience by the things which he suffered" (Heb. 5:8). If it was necessary for him, how much more for us. Man's rebellious spirit is a major cause of his deepest miseries.

At times we may be like the little boy whose mother had told him repeatedly to sit down. Finally, he obeyed, but looked up at her defiantly and said: "My outside is sitting down, but on the inside I'm still standing up!"

The rebellious heart not only experiences much unhappiness here but is unfit for heaven. Therefore, it is "for our profit" to learn submission to divine will now.

HARDSHIPS HELP US READJUST OUR SENSE OF VALUES

Sometimes we get our lives centered on the wrong thing, and the Lord does us a favor by shaking us to our better senses. Job felt that the Almighty "hath taken me by the neck, and shaken me to pieces" (16:12). When Jonah got on the wrong track, God gave him a good "whaling" which turned him back in the right direction. "In the day of prosperity be joyful, but in the day of adversity consider" (Eccl. 7:14). Consider what? Many things, for instance:

Illness causes us to consider the frail and temporary nature of our bodies. As we realize this more fully, we turn our thoughts to eternity and our soul's welfare. Pain and suffering can be used to develop patience, courage and a hope for something better.

Grief, losing a loved one, can draw us closer to heaven. The next world seems more real than ever before when a dear one waits for us there. This links our hearts to eternity, helps to remove the dread of death, and deepens our resolve to prepare for heaven.

Financial reverses cause us to consider the transitory nature of all material things and to realize our own limitations. The same blow which demolishes a man's business may build up his character, for it can cause him to lean more heavily upon the Lord. Then who would call it a misfortune?

Disappointment in friends and loved ones helps us depend more fully upon our heavenly Father. This was true of Job.

TRIALS INCREASE APPRECIATION OF LIFE'S JOYS

Once when Madam Shumann-Heink was asked to appraise the talents of a young singer, her comment was: "She has a remarkable voice and the promise of a wonderful career, but she will not attain her full power until she has experienced more of the sorrows and heartaches of life."

"Sorrow is better than laughter; for by the sadness of the countenance the heart is made better" (Eccl. 7:3). Adversity enlarges the heart, sharpens the sensibilities, and therefore increases one's capacity to enjoy all the sweet and noble and beautiful experiences of life.

> I have known sorrow — therefore I
> May laugh with you, O friend, more merrily
> Than those who never sorrowed upon earth
> And know not laughter's worth.
>
> — Theodosia Garrison

Why is this true? Until trouble comes, we cannot possibly feel the deepest need for our heavenly Father, our friends, our loved ones, and thus cannot fully know the joy and comfort of that need's fulfilment. Only when we look at the valleys can we appreciate the height of the hills, and without the valleys there would be no hills. Without the bitter, there could be no sweet — for one who has never tasted the bitter does not know how to recognize the sweet.

> Would we know that the major chords were sweet,
> If there were no minor key?
> Would the painter's work be fair to your eyes,
> Without shade on land or sea?
>
> Would we know the meaning of happiness
> Would we feel that the day was bright
> If we'd never known what it was to grieve,
> Nor gazed on the dark of night?

THE RAIN OF ADVERSITY NOURISHES THE FRUITS OF THE SPIRIT

Christ said: "Every branch that beareth fruit, he purgeth it, that it may bear more fruit" (Jno. 15:2). God sees that which is precious within his children, the purity and beauty possible after the purging is over; and thus he chastens because he loves. Have you ever seen a garden or vineyard overgrown with weeds and briars? You at once conclude that the caretaker no longer cares. The one who cares prunes here and cuts there, waters and digs — that his plants may flourish and bear more fruit.

The rain of adversity is part of the process which nourishes the fruits of the spirit. You remember the little song containing these words:

> **It isn't raining rain, you know;**
> **It's raining violets.**

Rain is necessary, if we would enjoy the beauty of the flowers and the sweetness of the fruit. Where showers fall most, the growth is greenest and most luxuriant. So when adversity comes, think not that it is raining pain, grief, despair and heartache. Think rather that it is raining love, joy, longsuffering, gratitude, patience, hope, faith and courage — for by adversity these fruits can grow more abundantly in your heart. We want to pluck the fruit, but have we so matured that we can thank God for the rain that must precede it?

Humility increases with hardships. Humility is a realization of our dependence upon God and fellowman. Paul said: "There was given to me a thorn in the flesh . . .lest I should be exalted above measure" (II Cor. 12:7).

Patience is developed through tribulation: "Tribulation worketh patience" (Rom. 5:3). The dictionary defines patience: "the power to wait calmly; to endure or persevere." Someone has defined it: "the ability to idle your motor when you feel like stripping your gears." Disraeli said: "Patience is a necessary ingredient of genius." Patience must be learned, for impatience is a natural trait of childhood — exemplified by the little boy who planted seeds and then dug them up every morning to see whether they had sprouted.

Patience is the attribute most generally associated with Job, for it is cited in the New Testament: "Behold, we count them happy which endure. Ye have heard of the patience of Job, and have seen the end of the Lord; that the Lord is pitiful, and of tender mercy" (Jas. 5:11). As we study Job's life, we see him manifest impatience with his friends and even at times with God. However, "the trying of your faith worketh patience" (Jas. 1:2-4). Through his trials, he learned more patience. He endured until he saw "the end of the Lord; that the Lord is pitiful, and of tender mercy."

Many years ago a prisoner condemned to life imprisonment carved on the walls of his London prison cell: "It is not adversity that kills, but the impatience with which we bear adversity."

Faith can be increased by tribulations. Job, known for patience, became impatient with God. Why, he demanded, was he so tormented? Instead of answers, he received questions. Finally, to replace his questioning, came trust. He said: "Now mine eye seeth." With the eye of understanding, he saw things he had never seen before. After severe trials, Christians have oftentimes said: "I have read a certain Scripture many times, but only now do I understand what it means." This confirms our faith, for we see that our heavenly Father knows the answer even before we face the problem. Sometimes we pray for more faith, when in reality we are not wanting a stronger faith but rather a change from faith to sight. Job learned to walk by faith and not by sight, to trust when he could not know. This is what made him the model sufferer of all time.

Hope is more precious than ever after the torment of trials: "Tribulation worketh patience; and patience, experience; and experience, hope" (Rom. 5:3,4).

Gratitude can grow more abundantly in the heart that has known hardships. One who has been near death can more fully appreciate the daily gift of life. One who has been separated long from loved ones can be more thankful for the joy of being together. One who has lived for days on nothing but cornmeal mush can be more grateful for a good steak than the person who has never been through such an experience.

Sympathy means "to feel with." God sympathizes with us and comforts us, not just to make us comfortable, but to make us comforters (II Cor. 1:3-7). It is not possible to "feel with" another's woes until one's own heart has bled. Sympathy has been defined as two hearts tugging at one load. Who among your friends is most skillful in binding up wounds and drying tears? Most likely someone who has suffered much. So it is with you. If the storms and the battles have left you weary and wounded, then sympathy is enlarged in your heart; and you will be able to comfort the storm-swept and the battle-scarred. Heartaches have given you the privilege of touching other lives with benediction. You are more able to "bear ye one another's burdens" (Gal. 6:2).

Longsuffering, tolerance and understanding of other's failures and woes are then increased in the heart, for these are actually forms of love and patience and sympathy. One can more easily be "kind one to another, tender-hearted, forgiving one another" (Eph. 4:32). Our responsibility is not so much to see through each other as it is to see each other through. This was thoroughly understood by the preacher who kept before his congregation this motto: "Let's help each other to heaven."

HARDSHIPS HELP ATTAIN THE MOST NOBLE ACHIEVEMENTS

Many of life's blessings can be obtained only by what seems to be destruction. The wheat must be crushed if the bread is to be enjoyed. The flower must be crushed before it gives forth its sweetest perfume.

> As aromatic plants bestow
> No spicy fragrance while they grow;
> But crush'd or trodden to the ground,
> Diffuse their balmy sweets around.
> — Oliver Goldsmith

Likewise, most of the world's masterpieces were nurtured in the soil of adversity and born from burdened hearts — in literature, art, music and other fields. Intense trials seem to be a necessary part of the preparation for great achievements. Throughout the ages, even to this present day, God has trained his rarest scholars in the school of adversity. From seeming defeats have come the most notable victories. From the caves of refuge came some of David's sweetest psalms. On the ladder of unjust treatment, Joseph climbed to the top of the Egyptian government and ever closer to the heavenly Father. The world's greatest victory — Christ's triumph over death and the grave, came after the world's severest trials — Gethsemane, the cross and the darkness of the tomb.

Job was crushed beneath the heel of adversity, but from this seeming defeat came two glorious victories: (1) *He was blessed by the trial.* Though "perfect and upright," through trials he gained a deeper spiritual insight and a treasure more precious than gold — a faith tested and proved, ready to be "found unto praise and honour and glory at the appearing of Jesus Christ." (2) *His victory blessed all mankind.* The dark days in which he wrestled with humanity's most bewildering problems are the only days which make him worth remembering. But for them, his name probably never would have been recorded in history's annals either sacred or secular. Because of them, you and I can be strengthened and encouraged.

REVIEW EXERCISE

1. What is more precious than gold? ....

2. Why does God chasten his children? ....

....

3. Christ "learned .... by the things which he ...."

4. What did Peter say when he began to sink? ....

5. "In the day of prosperity be ...., but in the day of adversity ...." Scripture: ....
6. Paul said: "We had the sentence of death in ourselves, that we should not .... in .... but in God which raiseth the dead." Scripture: ....
7. "By the sadness of the countenance the heart is ...." Scripture: ....
8. In Christ's parable of the vine and the branches, a branch represents a Christian. What does Christ say will happen to every branch that bears fruit? .... Why? ....
9. What "worketh patience"? ....
10. One reason God comforts us is: "that we may be able to .... them which are in ...." Scripture: ....

FOR THOUGHT OR DISCUSSION

1. Many times we become impatient because God does not grant our requests. Have we ever thought about how patient he is with us, how many times he has to wait for us to do as he has instructed?
2. When Peter was an impetuous young man, perhaps he would have doubted the value of sorrows and trials. However, as he grew older and as the Holy Spirit guided him, his writings emphasize the certainty, the necessity, the nature and the value of testings. It would be a profitable study to go through his writings and make a list of all teachings on this subject.
3. God speaks of the lasting influence of a godly life: "their works do follow them" (Rev. 14:13). The following words of Henry Ward Beecher apply not only to Job but to many other righteous men and women:

   When the sun goes below the horizon it is not set; the heavens glow for a full hour after its departure. And when a great and good man sets, the sky of this world is luminous long after he is out of sight. Such a man cannot die out of this world. When he goes, he leaves behind much of himself. Being dead, he speaks.